IN SEARCH OF THE FUN-FOREVER JOB
Career Strategies That Work

Ellis Chase

bacon press books
washington dc

Copyright ©2013 Ellis Chase

All rights reserved. No part of this publication may be reproduced, stored in a retrieval system, or transmitted by any means — electronic, mechanical, photographic (photocopying), recording or otherwise — without prior permission in writing from the author.

This publication is a product of the author's experience and opinion. It is sold with the understanding that the author and publisher are not engaged in rendering legal, accounting or other professional services. If legal advice or other expert advice is required, professional services should be sought.

The opinions in this book are solely the author's and do not reflect on any organization he is affiliated with. The stories and clients used in this book are composites; all names have been changed to protect confidentiality.

Some of the material has previously appeared in *The National Business Employment Weekly/Wall Street Journal*, Columbia Business School e-newsletter, Vault.com, and Columbia Business School Career Opportunities Information Network.

Published in the United States by Bacon Press Books, Washington, DC
www.baconpressbooks.com

Editor Lorraine Fico-White
www.magnificomanuscripts.com

Cover and Book Layout and Design: Stephanie Smith and Allie Tucker
www.143Creative.com

Cover Photo: © 2009 Ljupco
Author Photo: © 2012 Amanda Siegelson

ISBN 978-0-9888779-2-4

Library of Congress Control Number: 2013933916

PRINTED IN THE UNITED STATES OF AMERICA

6/21
Soc.
4

For Carola and Hannah, who have made my life fun-forever

TABLE OF CONTENTS

Preface

The title of this book came from my daughter who, at age eight, wrote and illustrated a "book" called *When I Am Grownup.* I'm not sure that most eight-year-olds would be concerned about professional choices or involved in much self-reflection, but she was the daughter of a career consultant and a psychoanalyst and could hardly avoid this type of thinking. It was genetically predetermined.

In her book, Hannah ruminated about her possibilities. She felt she'd want an "unushowoll" job "that I can do most anything I want in, something like the fun-forever job." She worried that such a job might not be available and considered other options (a headshrinker or a headhunter) but continued to feel concern about even those jobs working out.

What was particularly striking to me was that so many of my clients and students have expressed a similar wish for a totally fulfilling career, as if they hoped to discover their perfect, passionate calling out there somewhere.

The concept of a "fun-forever job" is amusing because everyone—including, perhaps, Hannah at age eight—knows that it's absurd. This does not appear to prevent people from wanting it anyway.

Of course there are a few lucky people who seem to have found that fun-forever job, or *think* they have, but the number of such people is indeed very small. A job means *work*, meaning on a daily basis, on most days of the week. Seeking consistent passion puts a heavy emphasis on something that is rarely achieved and often leads to disappointment and discontent at work. Of course, it's possible to love a job or be passionate about a career, but forever? That's like looking for a lifetime soul mate who's great looking, rich, witty, sexy, and sensitive—someone you'll feel excited about all the time for the entire relationship.

To some degree, the search for the fun-forever job has continued for Hannah, as it has for many of my clients, although they refer to it in different terms. Sometimes, it'll be "something totally exciting," and other times it's as basic as "something I won't dread every day."

I believe career development should be a process that includes figuring out what works and doesn't work, clarifying personal values, understanding personal style, and leveraging that knowledge moving forward. It doesn't have to be a lifetime decision. Sometimes it may mean that your job only needs to be reasonably good if it supports you and provides you with a salary, security, and benefits, and you can gain the passion part from what you do outside your job. Or you might turn your full-time job into a part-time one and work on several different activities outside of your core job. There are many other permutations; the key is to not put the pressure of the Big Decision on yourself too early and to realize it may take some time to develop a career that suits you.

My own career path, as I explain in Chapter 1, is a good example of the many twists and turns you may need to take to reach that point. I've written about my own experience in the hope that others who find the career development process complicated or painful may understand better that it often involves a series of realizations and changes—sometimes even circling back to what you knew in the first place.

A note about the statistics in this book. Throughout my career, and now at Columbia Business School, I have followed the business journals, management company surveys, and data from the Bureau of Labor Statistics, to name just a few sources. The statistics I use represent the figures that are most widely accepted in career management. As I mention elsewhere, job search is not a science. Neither is gathering data on how those searches are conducted.

In Search of the Fun-Forever Job is meant for anyone trying to decide on a career path or the next move, whether you're 22 or 52. I've gathered the best advice from my own experience and my 30 years of working with private clients and students. I hope the advice here will help to dispel the anxiety that naturally accompanies any career change so that you can make your job search more efficient, more effective, and more successful.

Ellis J. Chase
President, EJ Chase Consulting, Inc.
New York, New York
February, 2013

IN SEARCH OF THE FUN-FOREVER JOB
Career Strategies That Work

Chapter 1

Getting Personal

I've always wondered how people select their professions. Why did my friend become a teacher? Why did my sister-in-law become an advertising executive? Why did some have difficulty figuring things out for so long? How did others come to such quick conclusions so early in their lives? What were the personal characteristics and values involved in the decision-making process? What motivated some of my friends to become psychotherapists? Did they do it because they thought it would solve their personal problems? Was it born out of a desire to help, an interest in human behavior, or some complicated combination of factors? This curiosity applied to my own profession as well.

While some career advisors figured out early that they liked the idea of providing career help, most of the professionals I've known in the field have followed a circuitous route to get there, maybe even tortuous.

I fall into the latter category. I like to think those of us who have been through several changes—or as I would prefer to call them, evolutions—have put a lot of time into thinking through what we want to do professionally, we have acquired some insight into the thinking underlying these changes. That's on good days, when I believe the process is interesting and complex. But on other days, I think of my personal process as having been way too slow in developing, while I failed to pick up the obvious cues. Ultimately, I've concluded that regrets are a waste of time. The focus should be on whether you are pleased with where you are *now*, and if not, what can you do about it?

I think of career management as an evolutionary process that also involves a concept usually associated with religion —epiphanies. Career epiphanies. The blinding flash of light —aha! So *that's* what I should do (at least for that particular moment).

Many of the career management professionals I have known knew early on they wanted to help, wanted to make an impact. Some had been clergy, and some had worked in non-profits. Others were psychology majors in college, many with PhDs, who wanted to apply their training to business and careers, instead of more traditional clinical work. I fell into that category a little bit; I had worked during high school summers with emotionally disturbed children in several programs.

This book is not biographical. Rather, it contains thoughts and commentary that have developed over many years on various topics concerning career development. I thought it might be useful to discuss a few of my own evolutions and epiphanies to illustrate that most careers are not decided arbitrarily but are more organic.

In the 1970s' sitcom, *The Mary Tyler Moore Show*, a major character, Ted Baxter, loved to introduce himself to his TV audiences by saying, "It all started back in a small radio station in . . ." as though anyone was interested.

So, I'll skip over any irrelevant personal details and stick to the career issues.

All I ever was sure about was that I wanted to teach. From as early as I can remember, I recall sitting in classrooms thinking I could probably do that—better, funnier, and with more showmanship. Bad teachers drove me nuts because it seemed so obvious to me how they *could* have done it well.

I knew I wanted to teach; it should have been simple. Except for the complications. I was a serious musician with a strong interest in psychology as well. Yes, I was one of those previously mentioned psychology majors but I had no intention of becoming a clinician. In other words, I had majored in something that interested me, in which I had zero professional ambition. Or so I thought at the time. As it turned out, the psychology background actually played a key role in my later career choices. I did choose wisely for graduate school and obtained an MA in teaching secondary English, getting back to what I had always thought I would do.

And the slog began.

I became a junior high school teacher, working with an age group often considered the worst and most difficult for teachers. For some reason, I loved it. My wife thought it was because I was a perpetual 14-year-old myself but that's for another book. (She may have had a point.)

In those days, teaching jobs were in great demand because male teachers were able to get a draft deferral to avoid the Vietnam War. The best job I could get, in a very tight job market, was in a parochial school in Brooklyn. Not my top choice. This, my first teaching job, was initially like working on another planet. But I loved it. Smart, motivated kids made the whole experience satisfying. It affirmed everything I had always believed about teaching. Nevertheless, the money was terrible; I took on evening work teaching English in an alternative high school system, which served high school dropouts. This, too, was an exciting opportunity, and I realized pretty quickly that I not only loved teaching but the location, subject or level did not matter.

I moved from the parochial school to a private school on the Upper West Side, this time in high school, while continuing to work at the alternative school. In addition to teaching English and social studies, I added drama, which started a pattern I followed throughout the teaching part of my life—I'd volunteer for any subject. Loved this job, too.

In order to make more money (again), I found a full-time job in a private junior college, as part-time administrator and part-time teacher. I taught English, sociology, psychology, and, for a short time, Gregg shorthand, in which I always had to keep one lesson ahead.

At the same time, I worked with a cabaret singer as her accompanist, arranger, and conductor. Here was where the career story got complicated. She became successful, needing more and more of my time. Vacations from school meant going on the road with her to other parts of the country and Europe. I began to work with other singers as well, trying to balance two full-time careers simultaneously. This was manageable for a while. When asked about my career, I talked about the "day gig" and the "night gig" and about how these two careers were the two, complementary sides of myself.

They were indeed two parts of me, but somehow, neither of them was quite right. And they didn't fit together.

There I was, from my early 20s to early 30s, trying things out, which is what I think most young people should consider. (Of course, there are the exceptions for those who know early on exactly what they want to do.)

I knew that I loved the music, liked the rehearsing/ creating process more than performing but didn't like the lifestyle, the lack of structure, or the rampant narcissism that unfortunately went along with most of the singers I knew.

I also knew that I was a natural teacher, liked the people I worked with, didn't have difficulty with school bureaucracies (very lucky in that respect), liked that it offered some structure and flexibility, but I did not like the financial aspect.

None of it felt quite right and getting up at 6:00 a.m. to do the "day gig" and getting to bed at 2:00 or 3:00 a.m. after the night one wasn't going to work for very long. Being 28 wouldn't last forever.

A critical juncture occurred at this point. I knew that teaching was not going to provide me with enough income to live in Manhattan, and I was starting to get a little bored with some of the repetition. I continued with the music career, which was exciting, although I still did not enjoy the lack of control over the daily routine or the difficult personalities of the various people I worked with in a notoriously difficult and unstable business. While I realized that I could make a good living with the music, I didn't want to continue on a full-time basis.

I've found it incredibly useful to remember this period. Scary. Not quite sure of finding anything that would work in the long run. Learning how to do serious job searches and dealing with the isolation and uncertainty inherent in that process. Riding the emotional roller coaster. Characteristically for my profession, many of us have experienced these difficult periods and have some insight into what it's like to go through the process.

Back to my dilemma. I was clearly on the road to making a really bad choice out of desperation. Always a danger when the process takes too long. Anxiety takes over. But it was a choice that actually added a significant credential for later work. I landed a position with one of the big banks in staffing. Talk about different planets. I didn't even own a suit.

This decision was motivated by a need to make more money as well as add more structure (and maybe legitimacy) while continuing the music. I enjoyed the bank job, but I never felt comfortable in the culture. It took me five years to realize that it wasn't for me. I had little in common with my colleagues. Sometimes, I felt we spoke in different dialects. While a difference in background and education is sometimes a good thing, as diversity usually is, this one was tough for me to deal with; it presented too many disparities. When I spoke about my night gig, I received strange looks and a complete lack of interest. My division managers discouraged me from ever mentioning it again. Clearly, this was not the right environment. Ironically, I liked the work and learned a great deal about how companies hire and how employees move inside an organization.

As mentioned before, sometimes I'm a little slow on the uptake. By the end of the fourth year or so, I began to look for another position, mistakenly (again) in other big banks. I finally realized that most of those cultures were not for me; it wasn't just the organization where I had been working.

One day I was networking with a perceptive woman in a big bank. Somehow, she picked up that I genuinely liked the part of my job involving career development/internal mobility. She also noted that I particularly enjoyed explaining hiring methodologies to the various divisions and training the managers in interviewing techniques. Teaching! She suggested I look into the then-burgeoning field of outplacement consulting firms. I had no knowledge of the field because the bank where I worked had its own internal outplacement function. (Employees referred to it as "The Aloha Room.") The search took a long time. Although I had the credentials, I was perceived as too young. (I wasn't.) This was a field that prized age and seniority. Eventually I figured out how to dress, look, and act older, which surprisingly helped a great deal.

After another long and difficult search (even more material for my future clients and students), I landed in a boutique consulting firm. This led to another job in the largest of all the outplacement consulting firms, where I became managing director of one of their offices.

The work was exactly what I wanted. It involved group work (teaching again), individual advisement, a strong component of helping, and a measure of psychology. There was significant creativity involved in program development and variety. Eleven years.

But something was still wrong. One more epiphany was needed. The other realizations involved figuring out what my interests really were, how they could be best utilized, what cultures were good fits, and where I could actually earn a reasonable salary with some incentive. What became increasingly apparent was that I needed more autonomy.

I find many clients approaching 40 realize they want to take more control over their daily routine. A consultant I met at the first outplacement firm said it beautifully. "I never want to work anywhere that I have to stay in the office on Friday afternoon with nothing to do."

For me, that time had long passed. I had little patience for big corporate bureaucracy. I wanted more control over what I did, day to day, without some remote authority dictating some new and/or ridiculous policy.

In addition, I was dealing with a new managing principal. For the most part, over the years, my luck with managers had been pretty good—terrific manager at the bank, non-interfering principals at the schools, and an excellent managing principal (still a good friend and professional associate) at the consulting firm. But she left, and her eventual replacement was one of those demanding bosses I now hear about every day from clients and students. She was prone to temper tantrums and unwilling to tolerate any difference of opinion. She sometimes took to throwing things at people with whom she disagreed. (I was definitely at the top of her list. I'm not kidding.) This in a human resources consulting firm? Where the primary clients were people in transition? It was a bad situation for everyone who reported to her.

Clearly it was time for me to leave for two reasons. First, I couldn't stand being in the same room with this woman, even on only a monthly basis. Second, I wanted more independence and autonomy.

The first task was easy because she resigned well before I did. I was glad that something got me moving, even if it was a difficult colleague. The second step took a while.

I wanted to go out on my own and take control over my own work life. The big question was—how does someone who is basically risk-averse launch an independent business?

The answer was to segue gradually out of the consulting firm by requesting a more part-time arrangement and slowly building a private practice.

It worked. My plan was to try about seven different activities simultaneously, more or less a "throw it against the wall and see if it sticks" business plan. They were related, all having to do with different aspects of career development.

At this point, it was time to find out how my personal network of many years would pay off. I'd like to say I was conscientious about maintaining relationships, but I wasn't that good at it. I did have some longstanding, solid relationships; those were the people I visited over the course of a few months. A key one was the head of the program at New York University where I had been an adjunct instructor for 19 years.

Most of our previous contact had been at the beginning of a semester, and this consisted of a quick call from her ("What do you want to teach next semester?" or "Would you speak at the open house event?"), which led to the logistics for arranging the next course or event.

She was at the top of my list as a perfect person to reconnect with. Good relationship, lots of contacts, good listener, and good advice. Over a long lunch, I explained my objectives and how I was going about my search. I asked for her opinion. (I was trying hard to follow my own advice.) Somehow, we ended up talking about my distant past as a teacher. She wanted to know why I liked teaching so much. It certainly was, as most adjuncts at universities can attest, not the money. As it turned out, this was a critical part of the conversation.

A couple of days later, a woman from one of the major accounting firms (now one of the Big Four; then one of the Big Eight) called and asked if I'd be interested in consulting in the firm's summer internship program. She was having great difficulty finding someone who had experience in teaching inner city students *and* was an experienced career counselor. Talk about coincidences. She had called my friend at NYU, searching for a person who fit that unusual profile. (As I'll explain later, good networking technique frequently not only involves reaching out to multiple contacts but also involves having some good fortune, too.)

This led to a consulting job for the next five summers—my first major corporate consulting as an independent. This was pure good timing and the result of keeping up a solid business relationship.

By the end of two years of being on my own, it became clear to me what would work, what I liked, and how the business would proceed. It's been a work in progress, but I will say at this point, 15 years in, that I've enjoyed it. Definitely the right decision. Finally.

One of the key pieces has been . . . teaching. In addition to my having been an adjunct at NYU, I have ramped that up at Columbia Business School—and other Columbia University colleges—since February 2002 as a retained consultant, where I've had the opportunity to help build programs, teach in them, and advise individual students. The big picture is now made up of a combination of private practice advising, executive coaching and training in corporations, and the work at Columbia.

Yes, it's been a slow, sometimes frustrating process, but absolutely worth it. I now have autonomy, upside, flexibility, interaction with a variety of cultures, changing schedules, a self-imposed structure, and . . . teaching. All the key ingredients are there. Figuring out how to fit the variables together has been the critical factor. Fitting the career to the life, rather than the other way around, has been a major evolution and one that I talk about with clients.

Chapter 2

The 30,000-Foot View: Career Transition

Career transition is daunting. While any life change is tough, professional moves involve choices that may dominate or define your life. How to do it? Where to begin? How to get organized? How to keep on an even emotional keel and deal with all that rejection? What techniques will be the least painful?

Notice that I said "least painful" and not "most comfortable." I'm not one of those career advisors who think this endeavor is a wonderful self-exploration or some kind of self-expression. It's job search, involving a great deal of rejection and exposure to all sorts of bad behavior. It's not pleasant, except when it's over.

I'd guess that most people start with . . . panic. Anxiety. Fear. When I meet private or corporate clients or business school students, I often hear, "I don't know what I want to do, and I should've figured that out years ago," or "I've sent out thousands of resumes and haven't heard a thing. This means the job market is even worse than I thought."

These comments say to me, "I have no clue about how to do this." That's probably because most people have never really learned how to do it right. There isn't a comprehensive course in high school or college on career development, so why should anyone know how to proceed? While some lucky people are natural self-marketers or discovered their careers very early in life, most of us aren't in that category.

What follows is a general outline, from the 30,000-foot view, to give you some idea of what's involved in a successful job search.

Beginning—Assessment and Research

The words usually associated with beginning a career transition are "assessment" and "research," terms that might cause your eyes to glaze over, with a wish for a quick interview and job offer. Yes, a library might be necessary. And yes, assessment and research activities don't automatically yield direct answers. But wouldn't you rather do the heavy lifting of researching your options first, before you begin a search or make a firm decision? Successful career transition is all about making smart decisions.

A self-assessment can sometimes involve testing—maybe a Myers-Briggs Type Indicator (MBTI)—if you'd like to know more about what your personal style is and where the best stylistic fits might be or a Campbell Interests and Skill Survey. For business school students and alumni, Career Leader is an excellent assessment, measuring interests against hundreds of thousands of people with similar backgrounds and education.

The downside of assessment tools is that many who take them interpret them too literally. For example, if the Campbell indicates that you have a lot in common with people who like to work outdoors, it doesn't necessarily mean you should be a farmer. It may just mean that you like to go camping, something more avocational than vocational. If the Myers-Briggs says you have a mild preference for extroverted situations, this doesn't necessarily mean you should be in sales or that you want to hang out with coworkers all the time at the job. Many of the people I've worked with on interpreting these instruments have found them illuminating and even fun. The Myers-Briggs, for example, is non-judgmental and if interpreted well, can help in providing useful insights into many career issues such as type of organization desired (if an organization is being considered at all), work styles, interpersonal needs, and conflict resolution styles. It can also give you a better understanding of what personal development issues need to be addressed.

The upside of the well-researched, statistically reliable instruments is that they can serve as a basis, or at least a starting point, for career decisions. What they will not do is provide a recipe, as one of my colleagues at Columbia Business School always likes to point out. This process is not, unfortunately, science (or cooking). It's more art, and the assessments can provide a bit of a scientific basis for decision-making. Many people might want an assessment or a person to tell them exactly what to do, but this is your life, and it's complicated. These decisions are evolving, fluid, and may take a while.

If you are having difficulty narrowing down your options, you might try the "options exercise," which is to write down every idea you've been considering. Include the ideas that you think are crazy. Always wanted to dance? Hey, write it down! Then, list all the pros and cons of each idea. It's amazing what seeing all the pros and cons on paper will do. Patterns will start to emerge that weren't clear during your ruminations. The dancing option, while probably not feasible (since you had to have started training at age six), may suggest something about your general style and career preferences. Maybe it won't, but let's get everything on the table at this point. Everything that's on your mind about careers might yield a clue. Your goal will be to narrow the options down to two or three reasonable ideas. They don't have to be definitive; they're what I like to call baseline ideas. A good baseline idea is one where you think you have a better than 50% buy-in. It will serve as a beginning point, not a decision, at this early stage.

Ideally, you will have two or three baseline ideas you can use to build your due diligence research and your personal contact network in order to validate your ideas, find out whether or not they're feasible, and determine if there's a market. These ideas will also help you figure out what your strengths are and if you have any gaps in experience or skills, so that you can rationally decide which of these options might be worth pursuing. Better yet, it would be great if during this process, you discover that there are ideas you hadn't thought of before.

Don't forget to include your personal values. Where does money fit in? What's your "drop dead number?" I don't mean you should say that to anyone who offers you a job. Rather, it's what your absolutely bottom number is. What kind of people do you want to work with? What size organization do you think you'd prefer? Do you want lots of autonomy or a highly structured environment? Or do you want an organization at all? Perhaps you would prefer working remotely or at home? Are you entrepreneurial?

I suggest to my clients and students that they make a list of everything that's important to them, including what they think might be inconsequential, even if the list is long. Then, after it's completed, asterisk those items where it would be tough to compromise. This is a great way to start a transition—you're already figuring out what's important to you before the difficult search wears you down and leads you to make too many compromises in order to end the process fast. Of course, there will be some compromise but . . . not too much if you're going to make intelligent career choices.

Several years ago, I had an unhappy attorney for a client. He insisted he hated practicing law; he wanted to leave his law firm so that he could set up a bait and tackle shop in Tahiti. He was completely serious. Talk about escaping! I had a tough time getting him to move off this idea as he actually had done a substantial amount of due diligence on this fantasy. We finally reached a point where he agreed to investigate other options. (Please note this was not a value judgment about anyone wanting to set up such a business, but this idea was totally wrong for this client. On the other hand, I usually dismissed the notion when anyone mentioned opening a B&B in New Hampshire. People always have this idyllic idea of what it would be like and are quite mistaken. It's killer work.)

He listed his options—pros and cons—along with personal values, and it became clear after much consideration that the problem was not the practice of law. It was the practice of law within a law firm. Not a structure guy, he needed clearly defined objectives. He also didn't do well with time constraints and preferred working in a collegial environment. At both of his previous firms, as in many law firms, he worked on his own. He eventually figured out that he would be happier using his skills in a corporate environment, for a variety of reasons that he'd pinpointed on his options and values lists.

He was what I called a "burn victim," a person who had been burned by working in the wrong culture in the wrong kind of job. (He wouldn't have been happy in Tahiti either.) He became highly successful in the new environment, securing a major promotion within his first year. The transition was based on a change of environment, not a change in career.

Once you've narrowed down those baseline ideas (career ideas that seem possible), researching involves finding out what organizations or resources exist for those options. For example, if you're looking into media marketing or business development in one geographical area, it's important you identify all the organizations in that area engaged in that business. You don't want to focus solely on the big name organizations, such as giant media companies like Time Warner or Viacom or Disney because that's what most of your competition is doing. You want to cast a wide net and find the smaller organizations, too—the ones creating new types of media or providing content to the larger organizations.

The tools for research can be found in any good business library. I'm a big fan of online media research like Factiva; it tells you not only which organizations are in any given area but also what the media have been writing about each company for the past year. This information is more valuable than just checking a 10K report or a company website. Always stay current. Read the business section of your local paper. Read *The Wall Street Journal*, if that's appropriate. Read the business magazines or the trade monthlies. Sometimes a professional publication, like *Advertising Age*, is the source of great information even for people who have nothing to do with advertising. Find out who's doing what and what the trends are. This will prepare you for your networking and interviewing later on and make you appear like the consummate insider, which is an important objective of this process.

Join professional organizations, alumni groups, or LinkedIn groups. Not only are organizations fast network builders but they're also a source of current information. LinkedIn has become an imperative in transitions. Learning how to navigate it is not difficult; if you need help, you can find resources online.

Your goal is multiple offers. Think of the process as being like a funnel. If you start off with 200 hypothetical jobs you would want and you research the organizations well, build networks into them, and uncover maybe 5–10 possible opportunities, you should end up with multiple offers. Of those 5–10, maybe a few turn out to be unfunded or unapproved; maybe a few turn out to be dead ends—no returned phone calls, even after multiple interviews. (Welcome to the wonderful world of job search.) You may come in second on an offer— actually a good thing, since it indicates you're executing your process well. You may end up with two or three offers. You can turn one down, which always feels great. Face it— you'll be dealing with an awful lot of rejection in this process, so it should be exhilarating when you get to be the one who does the rejecting. And then maybe you have the good fortune of playing one off another to get the offer raised. The key is that the statistical probability of success is dependent on a large beginning sample.

One last thought about research. Try to build a critical mass of information. Don't trust just one person or one source and then continue with your search based on that one piece of information. Frequently you'll find people give information that's easy—I like to call those people lazy and stupid—because saying "there are no jobs out there" is easier than brainstorming about possible ways to get those jobs. And that negative assertion is usually not true. One negative opinion, either in a newspaper or via a networking contact, can be misleading. If that opinion is borne out by others, then maybe it is true, but at least you've researched it through more than one opinion.

Proactive or Reactive

Not a tough choice when you learn the statistics. Practically every employment survey we rely on at Columbia shows that a proactive search, which essentially means active network building, is what works. Most of these studies show that approximately 80% of career transitions are successful through some form of proactivity. Everyone who embarks on a transition has one wish: the process will take a short time. Along with that wish comes the desire to get the job by using traditional, reactive methodologies—answering ads and contacting recruiters. You send the resume; they do the work. Unfortunately, according to the Bureau of Labor Statistics, the reactive techniques count for a very small proportion of the available jobs out there. It's surprising for many people to learn that ads and recruiters together might account for only 13% or less of the overall market. That includes all the new digital technology. Nothing has really changed in this regard for a long time now.

So why bother with these techniques? If, say, 13% (a generous estimate) of jobs are obtained through ads and recruiters, why spend a great deal of time on techniques that end up making you feel bad because of the lack of response?

Proactive job search means building networks, whether it's person by person, through LinkedIn, or through that wealthy relative. All are forms of networking. You may succeed, however, with a shortcut and avoid the heavy lifting. Lightning does strike every now and then, right?

Self-Marketing Tools

Once you've established and researched those baseline ideas, then networked for information to find out about your feasibility, it's important that you develop a Plan A and a Plan B and maybe a Plan C as well. I'll refer back to these as your targets.

Now you're at the point where you need to build marketing tools to support those plans. The two-minute pitch is the basis of effective self-marketing. It not only serves as a response to, "Tell me about yourself," but also serves as the foundation for approach emails, follow-ups, introductions at professional events, responses to a phone screen question, and establishing connections and self-branding on a new job. What you want to avoid is simply reciting your resume. The two-minute pitch is a marketing statement, not your personal record. I go into greater detail in Chapter 5, but to touch on it here briefly, the pitch should include these five components:

* A label or positioning statement

* Two or three skills or experiences that support the first item

* A unique selling proposition

* A list of current and past employment

* A recap

You'll need a good resume, obviously, but a resume is probably the most overhyped aspect of career transition. Yes, it's important to showcase your credentials and work history, but it's really not that hard. Way too much time is often spent on this.

Funny thing about resumes—everyone seems to have strong opinions on the subject, but often they contradict each other. Two pages. One page. Education on top. Education on bottom. Hobbies. No hobbies. Health status. (No!) And so on. Don't take all the opinions too seriously. What's most important about resumes is that they form the core of your self-marketing, along with the two-minute pitch, and provide a script for networking and interviewing. You need to find a style that's comfortable. For you. Then, you run it by either a knowledgeable friend or professional to learn what to tweak, edit, and reformat. After that, you test it with professionals in your target market. A resume is a small part of a comprehensive career transition. Here are a few suggested guidelines:

- Make the resume easy to read. Lots of white space on the page creates visual appeal. Use short bullets. Paragraphs should not be longer than four or five lines. Leave out the traditional "references available upon request." What are you going to say—that they're not available? Of course they're available. Why bother saying it?

- Do not include your objective. Objectives have been out of style for quite some time now. A resume should state what you are, not what you want. An objective is presumptuous.

- Include a summary, if it's appropriate for your field. Summaries are intended to be a distillation of what will be your two-minute pitch and will quickly explain, right on top of the resume, exactly what you are professionally, your skill sets, and how you're positioning yourself for your next career move. There are many types of summary statements —the short paragraph, the bulleted skills, and the more extended versions. Sometimes a summary is unnecessary. For example, some Wall Street professions require a quick one-page resume, no summary, with a clear, skill-oriented sequential work history, and in some cases, a second page that's a deal sheet.

- Leave out hobbies/interests in an "Additional Relevant Information" or "Other" section. Early in a career, that information can pad out a resume and provide some fodder for interviewing, but later in a career, my take is it's not all that important if you participated in intramural basketball in college. Sometimes, though, those extracurriculars actually might help. If you were an Olympic athlete or a musician in a recent production off-Broadway, that might be good item to list. But "avid reader" or "loves to eat" just doesn't do it. If you have skills to sell, sell them and leave the rest out. Include the languages you may speak fluently or conversationally or the unusual technological skills you possess, but omit the fraternity presidency. "Microsoft Word" as a skill is not particularly impressive, unless you're applying for a clerical position.

- Don't overdo revising. Once you've researched your market and validated your targets, give the resume a rest. Many job seekers end up changing and reformatting the resume for hours and weeks, and sometimes I think that's a way to avoid the real work of search, which is getting yourself out there and in front of decision makers.

- Don't automatically offer your resume. Sending out thousands of resumes, unsolicited, is not a job search. It's deforestation and not an effective strategy. Or even close to one. Resumes will not, as many say, get you "in the door." It's quite the opposite; unsolicited resumes will usually screen you out, for one reason or another. Here's a good strategy: only give out your resume when it's requested. Otherwise, you're just another job seeker, and you want to separate yourself from the pack. The best way to do this is not to lean on the piece of paper but to lean on your own personal presentation, with the resume as a support or leave-behind.

Networking

This is one of the most misunderstood concepts in career development. The basic problem is that people in career transition think networking means calling up everyone they know and asking if they know about job openings. This does work occasionally, but we're after larger numbers, with a far more subtle approach.

It's important to understand that the objective is to avoid feeling you're approaching people, hat in hand, begging for a huge favor. Good networking technique is a two-way process. Frequently, there's just as much in it for the other person as there is for you. The primary fear is, "Why should anyone—least of all a stranger—want to see me?" or "I hate feeling beholden to people or asking for favors." Despite all the negative associations, statistics still show overwhelming success with the use of networking techniques. These networking techniques will be covered in detail in Chapter 3.

Interviewing

Learning how to effectively interview is one of the more concrete aspects of transition. Although I cover the basics in Chapter 5, here are four key components when taking a look from the 30,000-foot view:

1. The match between the organization and you

It's critical to know as much as possible about the culture of the prospective workplace. What's the history? How well is it doing now? How much can you learn about its unique characteristics? The media research mentioned earlier is an excellent resource. Finding out what's been written about the organization is more informative than what you can determine just from the organization's website, which is a marketing tool for the organization. You should not only learn about what the company wants you to know, via its website, but also about what other sources are saying. The combination of website, media research, and database descriptions (Dun and Bradstreet, Hoovers, Standard and Poor's, etc.), along with your personal network whenever possible, can give you a pretty good idea about an organization or a key leadership person. It will also prepare you to ask questions that reflect your knowledge of their industry and/or organization.

A few years ago, I did a brief presentation at the Recruiters' Day at Columbia Business School. Approximately 100 organizations were represented. I asked the group what they thought our alumni and students could improve most in their interviewing. They answered that applicants should learn more about the organizations where they were interviewing. These recruiters reported that many applicants gave just a basic, generic presentation with no thought to the person on the other side of the desk. I was startled by this because I thought Columbia students and alumni were a very accomplished, sophisticated group, but I also realized that job applicants, frequently anxious and determined to get their agendas across, didn't always think about tailoring their responses to the situation.

It's also important to prepare by understanding how your skills and experience line up with what you know about the organization. An interview should not be a recitation of your entire work history; it's a marketing exercise, with you matching your skills and experience to what the job requires.

2. Proving your points

Once you've determined, as closely as possible what the job requires, you should prepare at least six two-minute "war stories" you can work into the interview. Yes, it's great to have excellent chemistry and show that you might fit into the organization, but it's more important to *demonstrate* that you can back up what you say.

3. Opening and closing

As outlined earlier, the two-minute pitch should be a major piece of the first five minutes of the interview. You want your branding out there as a strong opening and a linchpin for the interview—something to make it easy for the interviewer to understand you quickly.

But what about the ending? Most of my clients and students have reported that they have trouble with the ending of the interview, which can be awkward and uncomfortable for both parties. I think the closing should comprise two factors. One is asking what the next steps are in the process, and the other is a reiteration of a key marketing point and interest in the position. Don't just say "thanks" and leave. Use this moment as one last repetition of one of your key marketing points. "I'm excited about the opportunity because it seems that my background in _____ closely aligns with your needs. I'm looking forward to the next steps." Why not be a little assertive?

One more comment about proving your points. Employers like to hire enthusiastic applicants. They want to know you're excited about working with them. Show it. You might be anxious but that can be overcome. I like to see interviewing as performance art. It doesn't matter what you feel inside; it matters what you show.

4. Preparing the questions

Being well prepared for the actual substance of the interview is a major component for success. As I discuss in Chapter 5, there are only five questions that you need to prepare.

(1) Tell me about yourself (the two-minute pitch).

(2) Why are you looking for a job?

(3) Why should we hire you (the war stories)?

(4) Where do you see yourself in five years?

(5) How much are you looking to earn?

Marketing Plan

Creating a marketing plan turns what is essentially an unruly process into an organized project. It might include your targets (Plans A, B, and maybe C), market segments, research, networking contacts, and daily schedules. It will definitely include your marketing materials—outreach communications, resume, pitch, and follow-up emails. Staying organized helps you feel in control of a situation, even when that control is not always possible.

Record Keeping

Another way to stay organized and on top of things is to develop a simple record-keeping system. If you're adept technically, then an Excel spreadsheet will do fine. Don't fall into the trap of creating a sophisticated system that will take too much time to maintain. That's almost as bad as spending huge chunks of time refining a resume. My favorite system is to use 5x8 index cards, one for each contact. Everything about the contact should be on there, including the source of the referral, contact data, and detailed notes of whatever has transpired between you. Even a subjective comment or two will help in a protracted search, when you can't even remember the meeting. By subjective, I mean,

"This guy was an idiot," can be helpful to remind you that you don't want to waste too much time following up with him.

Review the notes (or cards) every day. It will automatically help you create your "to do" list for the next day and contribute to a sense that you have some measure of control. Plus, it prevents you from missing reminders that you were supposed to contact the person again in two months. Never let, "I'm too busy. Call me in two months." go by. When you call again, it'll be a great guilt motivator to remind the person on the other side of the desk that he/she asked you to call again.

It's amazing to me how many students and private clients have mentioned over the years that one of the best things I'd suggested to them was the record-keeping system. So much for all of the rest of my sophisticated and complicated advice, right?

The Emotional Roller Coaster

Emotions are probably the toughest part of transition. You're putting yourself out there. There is an incredible amount of random rejection. Maybe you've encountered condescension, been stood up, or received no response after a positive interview. I've found no lack of bad behavior stories in anyone's transition. There is a roller coaster quality to all of this, not to mention the isolation and the lack of concrete results for long stretches of hard work.

Maintaining a personal equilibrium and understanding that the roller coaster is part of the process will help you maintain your perspective.

Sometimes I feel like a personal trainer in my interactions with the people I'm advising because I'll always suggest some major aerobic activity during search as a great way to decrease anxiety. It also helps you maintain your appearance and your feelings of self-worth. During the worst search in my own professional life, I made running long distances an essential part of my daily routine. I actually look back fondly to that time, awful though it was, as the time I was in the best shape of my life. The structure was important for me as well. Transition is a challenge for anyone, no matter how qualified or solid you think you are. It's a disruption, and even the toughest will have some self-doubt along the way. Build structures for yourself that work well and make it easier to maintain a sense of control over a very difficult process. Take some time off—not too much as to interrupt momentum but enough to get away from the stress.

Speaking of momentum, this is another significant issue in the process. When I'm asked about how long it will take, my usual response is that it depends on several variables —clearly the market for the chosen targets but also your own discipline and consistency. Great technique, coupled with those factors, should work. Long disruptions or interruptions fueled by disappointment or rejection are tough to come back from. For example, if you're counting on one situation to pan out and stop all other activity, what happens if it blows up? You're stuck with no momentum, a terrible feeling, and the difficult task of starting again from scratch. Don't let that happen. Even if you have something so close that you already have a starting date decided, make sure you have more meetings planned until you receive an official offer letter. The process should be relentless with only a few periodic breaks.

Mastering these concepts will help dispel the anxiety of transition and make the process more manageable and successful.

Chapter 3

Networking: Not a Four-Letter Word

The concept is actually an indirect marketing approach to job search and information gathering, but I'm going to call it networking as a kind of shorthand. In general, while networking is fine for us to talk about in the office or maybe with family members, it's not an expression you want to use with anyone who can help you build your contact list. The term is off-putting, sounds exploitative and outdated, and may make the person you're contacting wonder, "How can I avoid this person who keeps calling and asking me for job leads?" We need to be a little more subtle. We could refer to "building information" or "researching your market" or any of a number of other accurate euphemisms.

I've learned from my practice that just the idea of indirect marketing can be a problem for people in career transition. While there are thousands of articles, books, and speeches about this subject, too often the advice makes the already anxious job seeker more anxious. Too much technique. Too much mush. Some people find it hard to accept that the techniques involved are *not* necessarily linear, they are not concrete, and they don't always work by themselves. In fact, you'll find networking works best when you use it in conjunction with all of the other search techniques. But the main point is that it does work. Except when it doesn't.

The Networking Nightmare

A great way to understand how to network successfully is to understand what can go wrong. This story is an extreme example.

Several years ago, I was approached by a career consultant. She sought to develop a relationship with the consulting firm where I managed a local office. She hoped there might be work for her in my office.

Her approach was poor on the initial telephone call. One of the first things she said, "I hear you know a whole lot of people from your activities in our professional association," told me right away that she wanted to exploit me. She made it clear our whole interaction was strictly about her.

I set up an appointment (I believe it's good business to meet people who approach you for informational purposes) and was pleasantly surprised. She had a great sense of humor (always important to me), as well as some excellent experience. And she had a unique skill—she was able to deliver group programs in two languages. It immediately occurred to me that she might be of interest to others in my company involved in a project that might require such a skill. I told her I'd contact my colleagues and put her in touch with them.

This is the best kind of networking—the kind you always want to happen—an immediate and direct result. It doesn't happen often, but when it does, the doors open faster.

I called the project managers, strongly recommending her, and both were interested.

She did not follow-up. No letter, no call. Not to me, not to them. I had spent time arranging introductions, which meant I now was in a position of owing a favor to the two people I called . . . and I looked foolish.

An interesting postscript to this story: she called me about six months later, with no acknowledgment of what had happened. Once again, she clearly was not thinking about the other person in this networking transaction. She said she was now ready to move forward with her plan and wanted to meet the people I had mentioned, as though I had been sitting for months waiting for her call.

Amazing. This time I did *not* make myself available to her.

The point to this story is that there must be a *quid pro quo* in all networking transactions, along with a keen sensitivity to the other person. The job seeker has to think, "What would it be like to be sitting in that chair? What would *I* think if *I* were being approached by this person?"

Getting Started

It is essential that you have your baseline targets (mentioned in Chapter 2) defined before you start to develop a network. Targeting is important because you want the people you're speaking with to have a clear perception of what your eventual goal is. You never want anyone to ask, "What is this person all about?" or "What do I do with this person?" This is true for both direct job search activities and information gathering/networking. In defining your target, you should include the type of industry, type of job, level of job, geography, culture of organization (or no organization, if that's your preference), work/life balance, and whatever other personal values are important to you at this beginning point.

Don't put pressure on yourself to come to immediate conclusions. Keep in mind this is just the starting point and you don't know where it's going to end up, unless you're quite certain at the start that you know what you want. I suggest to most of my clients they start with at least two or three of these baseline targets.

Questions you'll need to answer include: Where are the organizations? How do I become an insider, if I'm not one already? What do I need to learn? Would I be a viable candidate? Which of my skills are transferable and which aren't?

Some of the answers can be found by reading professional journals and magazines and performing online research. The rest will be discovered through direct interpersonal contact—networking.

Since, by most accounts and research, getting job offers through networking technique constitutes the vast majority of your total job possibilities, you're going to have to build a substantial contact list. Does this mean you have to be a back-slapping, "Yo, let's do lunch" type? Do you have to know the movers and shakers right away? Must you be highly social? Yes, of course it might help if you pursued that private equity career and Henry Kravis's nephew was your best friend in elementary school. Or it would be great if you were the type of person who went out every night and found it easy to meet people everywhere you went. (I knew an Executive MBA student at Columbia Business School a few years ago who was remarkably adept at this. He could go anywhere—including many local bars—and build new networks. His impressive connections all came from his ability to meet new people.) Or, perhaps your father is CEO of Time Warner.

But most of us are not like these people. We might know a couple of people who know a couple of people, and maybe we worked with someone who has all those relationships. Yet, we're still going to have to start somewhere. I suggest an "ABC" contact list.

- **The "A List"**

  This list includes: all of the people you know of who are a level or two above where you think you would be in the organization and function where you want to be; peer level, who could be valuable sources of information and possible access to those above you; and people familiar enough to you so that you can comfortably call them.

- ## The "B List"

This list includes all of the people in the "A List" *except* that you're not necessarily comfortable calling any one of them right away. Maybe there's someone you haven't spoken with in years and feel a bit awkward calling. Maybe there's someone you don't know that well and should write to first. Or perhaps there's someone you don't know at all, but you'd like to meet because you think you could learn significant information and perhaps build new networks. Or maybe there's someone you don't really like but you'd like to contact anyway.

This is the list my clients want to talk with me about the most because getting to the people they've named involves using the most difficult and complicated approaches.

- ## The "C List"

The "C List" consists of everyone else you know of who might provide connections to those who would be on an "A List" or "B List." How about the person who cuts your hair, your extended family, or your dentist? All of those people know others who may work in your targeted area. One of my favorite resources is college and graduate school—sometimes even high school—alumni associations. Alumni associations are particularly powerful networks for attorneys and MBAs. Those who were lucky enough to attend small private colleges will have access to a sort of private club—the college's alumni database. Membership in that club is a major motivation for gaining entry into many colleges, universities, and graduate schools. Even if you didn't attend an elite school, many other colleges and universities have well-established alumni organizations and alumni databases.

Professional associations are another favorite "C List" source. Join one (or more) in your target areas. Get on a committee. Two of the best committees are the membership and program committees. Why? In the first, you have access to the membership lists, and in the second, you can source and possibly meet key professionals in your field.

What about political or religious organizations? In this last category, I've found very few groups can match Mormons or Orthodox Jews for quick affiliation and building strong networks. I had two clients a few years ago who were Mormons, one living in New York City and one in New Jersey. They were able to build significant networks immediately through their church and extended family and friend affiliations. (One of them landed a terrific job in, of all places, Las Vegas.) I also had an American Orthodox Jewish client who lived in Jerusalem, and he relocated to Cleveland (don't ask) where he had never been and had no acquaintances. He built fast networking relationships through a synagogue there, despite not being especially assertive or outgoing.

Here's the good news. All you need is a minimum of five people after you've thought through your ABCs. Most job seekers will have more than that, but some—maybe introverted or recent arrivals to an area—will have a smaller number. Even if you only connect with two out of five, you will be able to build the beginning of a successful search based on referrals and information from those two. That's just the beginning.

The Three Philosophies

Don't worry. We're not going to discuss Kant or Hegel here. (After all, it's just a job search.) But I do believe there are three good ideas to which job seekers should subscribe.

1. Don't ask people directly for jobs or leads.

If you do your networking well, they'll figure out what you're trying to accomplish. Asking for a job or lead puts your contact into a corner. When you corner someone, it makes it difficult to get useful information. Instead what you'll get is someone trying to get out of that uncomfortable position, ending the meeting with you, and probably avoiding future contact as well. You also don't want to place someone in a yes/no situation. The odds of getting a good lead or knowledge of a good job at that particular moment are quite small.

We all hope for that lightning strike, which happens every now and then, but what you want from your contact is something that will lead to referrals, good information, job possibilities, and other leads. This is one area of networking where job seekers make a big mistake. They assume the purpose of the networking meeting is to ask for leads or jobs, to give a resume, and then wait for that lightning. It rarely happens that way. I've met many clients who are puzzled because they've had 50 or 60 meetings and no real job interviews. When we analyze the meetings, we frequently find that the clients used the "wham bam, thank you ma'm" approach to job search, which is to ask for a job or lead, leave a resume, and make no further contact. But with no further contact, you'll be forgotten in approximately five minutes– ten, if you were exceptionally impressive.

2. Understand what networking really is.

It's building new relationships or rebuilding old ones *over a period of time* so when your contacts hear of something appropriate for you, they'll remember you. What's important to remember in this definition is that the relationship develops over time, not overnight.

3. Give the process time to work.

Bruno Bettelheim, the late psychoanalyst and prolific writer, wrote that "maturity is the ability to delay gratification." I have always thought that was a great way to think about building networks. In other words, there are no shortcuts. You need to work the system to get the big payoff—job leads, job interviews, and offers. Successful networking takes time. It's a process, not a quick answer. For people who are anxious— perhaps frantic—about finding a new job, this is a very difficult concept to accept.

The Five Steps (plus . . .)

There are five critical steps in building networks. There are steps you can take beyond these five, but whether you will use them depends on how far you can take the relationship. (I like to call that point the "line of obnoxiousness," a moveable point where you feel you can't go any further with that contact. More about this later.) For now, let's say there are five basic steps, with the option for more depending on the situation. Steps one and two are interchangeable.

1. The email (or letter)

> This is a matter of personal style. There are people who love the telephone and can call anyone at any time. Since I'm not one of those (I don't even like making dinner reservations), I'll start with email. I think it's a good way to start the process because it doesn't blindside the recipient, and it can create a context for a follow-up call. For example, "This call is in regard to some recent correspondence . . ." In the email, you very briefly introduce yourself or mention the referral source, if you have one, and state that you're doing some research about your next job move. I suggest you stay away from any implication you're making a major change because that frequently scares people, as though they're not only going to have to explain too

much but also that you're not an insider. You always want to create the impression, even if you are making a radical change, that you're in some way one of them. An insider.

Next, briefly (there's that word again) explain who you are and that you're seeking a brief (again!) meeting to discuss industry trends, ask some questions, and explore possible new ideas. Suggest that perhaps you might be able to help each other in the long term.

Here's where we run into a problem. The question I hear from clients all the time is, "Why would this person, who is probably very busy, want to talk with me?" One answer is that sometimes it's a referral from a colleague. The other, and more important one, is that smart working people always want to build their own personal networks. Of course, not everyone out there understands the value of building professional networks. Many think it's a waste of precious time. We know better. People who build networks always have ready access for their own future job changes or other professional transactions.

One way to protect yourself from occasional rejection is to begin with the assumption that some of the people you try to connect with just don't get it. That's part of the process and means it's time to move on to the next person on your list. Understanding there's quite a bit of rejection in networking and all aspects of job search will enable you to maintain a good perspective.

Note: The decision about whether to use email or snail mail is not so easy. I sometimes urge the use of real, white stationery letters because they stand out. They're tactile, and it's not so easy to press the "delete" button on the other end. A few years ago, I met a recruiter from Microsoft at Columbia Business School. She suggested snail mail, which was a bit of a surprise. Her reason? She received way too many emails every day, and they all blurred together for her. The one or two pieces of regular mail she received per day made more of an impression. Remember, this is Microsoft we're talking about. The exceptions to my recommendation are when you're dealing with technology organizations (except for at least one person at Microsoft) or when you've already established an email connection.

2. The phone call

Sometimes people start with this step. I like the idea of following up the letter or email with a phone call so that the recipient expects the call. Telephone technique is a separate topic, but there are some key points worth mentioning here. As many professional sales people say, it takes an average of eight phone calls to get through to the person you want. That requires a great deal of fortitude and is certainly one of the hardest parts of networking. You need to learn some basic sales techniques. Here are a few tips:

- Use bulleted scripts (not word for word) so that very little will throw you off.

- Build relationships with gate keepers (the ultimate sales technique).

- Have a short version of your two-minute pitch ready at all times.

- Stand when you make your calls. It adds weight to your voice.

- Smile when you call. A smile is actually heard.

- Try hard not to leave your phone number in the recipient's voice mail, at least for the first few times you call. Say you will be "tough to reach" because you'll be in and out of your office during the next couple of days and that you'll call back. This way you avoid waiting for a return call and keep a bit of control over the situation.

- Leave short, direct messages.

- Try to avoid, whenever possible, having your meeting on the phone. A meeting in person creates more of an impression and memory.

- Don't give up too easily. Successful sales professionals (and you are definitely one of those in this process, like it or not) are relentless.

3. The meeting itself

It's been my experience that networkers put way too much pressure on the meetings; their expectations are too high. Many expect the meeting to yield instant job openings or leads, which is the exception, rather than the rule. I think there's a better way to look at it. Make the networking meeting about specific benchmarks. This also gives you a way to evaluate how useful the meeting actually was. The benchmarks could include:

- Building or rebuilding relationships. The overall purpose of building networks is not only to meet people, but also to make a relationship last over a period of time. A good approach and a good meeting aren't the end of the process. They're the beginning. Good business relationships, like good customer relationships, are built through a series of contacts. The benchmark here is, "Did you create the groundwork for a continuing relationship?" Sometimes, you also have to ask, "Do I *want* to continue this relationship? Will it be useful?" Not every person is going to get the same kind of follow-up. Don't go into automatic pilot in this process.

- Information and advice. This is how you create the structure for your meeting. Assuming that you've introduced yourself initially by giving a two-minute pitch/description of your background, there are two kinds of questions you should prepare: information questions that reflect that you know what you're talking about; and marketing questions, which is what you really wanted to ask all along.

The information questions signal that you've done some research on your contact's organization or you've done your own reading on the industry. (Research is a key element of your job search. Period.) These questions should suggest you're somewhat of an insider, even though you might be making a radical change. Coming prepared with questions shows you've made an effort to learn relevant information. What you don't want to do is appear to be a novice or make the other person do all the work.

Marketing questions also help validate your employability in your target areas. One great question to ask is, "How did you get to this point in your career?" That will frequently reveal some interesting twists and turns, giving you information you couldn't have known before. Other good questions along the same line are, "What do you look for when you hire here?" or "How does my background compare to people your organization hires?"

If you have five or six of these information and advice questions prepared for each meeting, the half hour you've requested should be filled (don't ask for more unless offered). As for the benchmark, useful information will certainly move your search along and help you refine it as you continue on to the next meetings.

- Names of more people to contact. Most people think this is the ultimate point to networking. It isn't; it's just one of several. But, if you do want to add to your contact list, it can be a very important component. A lot depends on how you pose the question. I suggest two ways. The first, asked at the very end of a meeting, is, "Could you suggest anyone I might speak with in the same way we're talking?" And if there's an immediate positive response, ask, "Would it be easier for you to make the introduction, or would it work better for me to call and use your name?" (Of course, you want the first option because it not only gives you a stronger referral but also gives you another excuse to call the referring person.)

Another technique, one I find highly effective, is to present a printed list of perhaps 25 targeted organizations with the organization you're visiting listed prominently. Ask what your contact thinks of the list, not if he or she knows anyone on it. That's too direct. Almost invariably, ego kicks in, and your contact will have trouble resisting the urge to say immediately, "I know the person who founded that organization, and I know the woman who runs their marketing and advertising . . ." and then you have some immediate referrals.

One of the reasons I know this technique works well is that I always fall for it myself when I'm on the other end of that question. Ego.

4. Follow-up thank you

As with interviews, the follow-up letter/email is

almost as important as the meeting itself. It's not just a courtesy; it's a marketing statement. In the letter, you will not only thank someone for the time, but you'll also recap some of the more interesting points you discussed. This is a positive reinforcement of the meeting, and will help to create the memory (a benchmark). You might also take the opportunity to add something you didn't get the chance to talk about like, "Oh, by the way, I thought you might also be interested to know I've had some experience in . . ." And there's that *quid pro quo* statement that you'd be glad to repay the favor in any way you can; the person should feel free to call on you at any time.

5. Follow-ups

This is where real business relationships happen, and where you will start to hear about opportunities, leads, and jobs. It is at this step (and 6, 7, 8, etc.) where job seekers too often drift away. But it is these steps, in addition to the steps outlined above, that create the relationship and memory which are so critical to this process. Here are some key ways to follow-up beyond the thank you letter:

- Let your contacts know that you've set up a meeting or have completed a meeting with someone they referred—thanking them again—and perhaps adding what was learned or accomplished.

- You've read a great article in your professional field and want to clip it and send it with a note to people you've met. The note might read, "Recently saw this, and thought you might be interested. Look forward to staying in touch..."

- You've got a quick email question about somewhere that you've interviewed.

- You would like to send an update on your progress. Here's where you might think you're going near the line of obnoxiousness, so be careful and think through whether the chemistry was good enough to go this far. And stay away from mass mailings. That's like announcing, "You're not that special; I'm including you in a large distribution . . ." (This is also a bad idea when you're letting people know you've landed a new job.) Definitely not a relationship builder.

- When you feel the relationship is solid or the chemistry is good (for example, the contact has emailed you back with helpful information or corroboration of a question), you might want to ask specific job search questions. These are judgment calls. You run the risk of stumbling over that line but it's one of the risks in the search. Just as you did with all other job search rejections or awkward moments, you'll pick yourself up and move on to the next person.

It's hard work, isn't it? Be sure to keep great records. If you lose control of your record keeping, you'll miss opportunities. If one of your contacts says, "I heard that XYZ Company is going to expand their IT function in a couple of months, and I'll be glad to introduce you to a friend of mine there," you'll make a special note of this. And when you do your daily review of all your notes, you won't miss this as the date approaches.

It's hard to ignore the statistical probabilities. Great networking technique will lead to multiple offers. It's definitely worth overcoming your awkwardness and discomfort. It's like the old New York State lottery ad campaign, "You gotta be in it to win it."

I've covered a lot of ground in this chapter. You may want to go back and reread it. But here's a quick summary.

- Start with an ABC contact list.

- Remember the three philosophies: don't ask directly for jobs or leads; understand what networking really is; and give the process time to work.

- Follow the five steps (plus . . .): the letter or email; the phone call; the meeting; the follow-up letter or email; and other appropriate follow-ups.

While you're following these steps you will want to create benchmarks so you can measure your progress. The benchmarks might include building or rebuilding relationships, gathering information and advice, and learning names of more people to contact.

And I can't repeat this enough—keep great records.

Chapter 4

Managing Your Personal Brand: The Critical Difference

One of the major surprises of my 11-plus years consulting in career management at Columbia Business School has been the realization that social intelligence is at least as important as any course of academic study, prior business experience, or superior skills. Many students think being smart, competitive, and goal-oriented will be enough. It's not.

We're constantly researching the components of success, trying to figure out how students can get an edge. In the various published lists we review, most do not include the "hard" skills. This in itself is surprising. The only so-called hard skill I've seen more than once is "prior experience." Many of the other top 10 critical skills for success in business include "soft skills" like active listening, conflict resolution, presentation skills, ability to work well in groups (playing nicely with others), willingness to embrace change, desire to learn, *and* for the subject of this chapter, general business/telephone/email/social media behavior.

In our presentations, to emphasize the importance of social intelligence, we point out that networking is everywhere, with a picture of George Orwell's Big Brother to clobber the point home. The message really is, "Creating a great general perception and building strong relationships should be a critical component of your success in business." Or, if we are thinking in marketing terms, "Social intelligence is part of creating your personal brand."

The Other Side of the Desk

I always like to ask my advisees, private clients, corporate clients, and students about the perception of the person "on the other side of the desk," or "What does that other person in the dialogue think about what you're saying and how you're behaving?" Many years ago, I heard this being referred to as *not* listening to radio station WII-FM (What's in It for Me?) and at Columbia we refer to this focus on the other person as WIFR (What's in It for the Recruiter?).

Another way of thinking about that other side is a concept from the 1980s called "spin selling," or "consultative selling." They all mean the same thing, which is thinking about what the other person is asking or explaining rather than focusing solely on your own agenda. The consultative selling point of view is great when, for example, during a job interview, you listen very carefully to the interviewer, and then respond by giving answers that person needs to hear, answers which build your value. What many in those situations do instead is recite their agenda, carefully prepared and rehearsed, but it frequently has nothing to do with what the person conducting the interview wants to hear.

People also make a first impression in the way they introduce themselves. Several years ago, I was involved with multi-week orientations at a major financial services organization. They emphasized the importance of employees introducing themselves to each other whenever they found themselves in the same room. This approach goes a long way toward building new relationships within the organization. That stuck.

The great handshake and direct eye contact are givens, right? Not necessarily. I've met many students who look elsewhere when speaking with you (sometimes due to a cross-cultural difference) or give the dead-fish handshake (a definite career killer). And what about names? Often people, particularly those with unusual names, will mumble their name fast just to get past this detail. That's a mistake. Don't you want to be remembered? Speak slowly. Make a joke about the name if necessary (rhymes with . . .) or restate it, acknowledging that it might be difficult to hear the first time. But don't minimize it. As someone with two last names, I'm used to people reversing them. Or not hearing the surname. I'll always say, "Chase, like the bank." And if called by my last name, I will remind them with a smile that it's the other way around.

Phones

Much research has already established that an inability to separate from one's iphone or Blackberry or 'Droid lowers productivity and creates a kind of artificial ADD. That's bad enough . . . but what about the effect on the others around you?

You need to think about what kind of perception you create when you're checking emails during a meeting, answering your phone at sensitive times, or inflicting your personal conversation on those around you. I'll never understand why a client answers the phone when the response to my call is, "I can't talk now because I'm about to go into the subway." Well, why did you leave the phone on if you can't take the call? This makes me not want to call again and sets a poor initial perception.

Obviously (and a lot of this thinking about telephone etiquette is indeed an exercise in the obvious), keep your phone off when in business or social situations, and don't create the perception that any incoming call or email is more important than the people around you. Also, make sure your voice mail message is clear and professional.

Email

Email can be a very effective tool in connecting with that other side. In the following email, however, the sender is making a clear, specific request, with an obvious agenda.

I want a job in general management.

Resume to follow.

The tone of the email is demanding, abrupt, and not likely to lead to building a relationship as part of a good business transaction. It's all about "I want." The recipient is simply not a factor in this communication. No salutation, no closing, no follow-up, no acknowledgment of the recipient. Just "here's what I want." The recipient thinks twice about it and doesn't feel especially receptive because of the poor communication style, even if the candidate has valuable skills.

Here's an example of an email that accomplishes what the sender intended:

Hi Ellis,

Thanks for confirming the appointment. Very much looking forward to talking with you and to kick-starting my process. I've completed the assessments and attended some of the lunchtime classes, and so far what I've learned confirms what I've been thinking: I might want to consider leveraging my healthcare background into some kind of marketing role. Not sure how to get started with all of that and was hoping to get a bit of an overview from you.
See you Friday!

Sincerely,
Meg Griffin

The writer of this email is thinking about creating a solid business relationship; the recipient is more likely to have a positive perception of the person, even before meeting her. Her brand is already established. She's been responsive, friendly, and clear in communicating the purpose of the meeting, making it easier for the sender to get more out of the interaction. It seems so obvious, but these little things do make a huge difference.

Email tone can be lethal. It can be misinterpreted easily. Despite the temptation to dash off emails quickly, it is important to pay close attention to what you are communicating.

Here's an example of an email that should never have been sent:

Debbie,

I CANNOT BELIEVE THAT IT'S THURSDAY AND THIS STILL ISN'T RESOLVED. As of last Friday you told me you were working on the wording of ONE sentence—WHAT HAPPENED that would make us lose an ENTIRE WEEK? I didn't think I needed to tell you how important this project is for Management —SO I'm telling you NOW. Losing these days will DELAY the results to

Management. I AM STRESSING TO YOU THAT THIS MUST BE RESOLVED SOONER THAN IMMEDIATELY!! EXPEDITE approval so that John can start pulling names TODAY!!! PLEASE do not delay this further.

Mary

This email was mistakenly copied to me by a private client. There are so many things wrong, it could form the basis of an entire Management 101 course about "what not to do" as a manager. But we're going to focus on the tone. Using caps in emails tends to communicate anger, which is inappropriate in any business communication. As I mentioned, the major problem with this email is that it should never have been sent in the first place. It's an accusatory, threatening email, and there's no way it will accomplish its purpose of getting the subordinate to do her job better. Rather, it will push the employee into a defensive corner. It would be more effective to discuss these concerns in person. The email ultimately does more damage than good. It either creates or reinforces a negative, unproductive tone.

I recently received another problematic email:

do you offer life coaching
where are you located

thanks,
Marianne

Back to the other side of the desk. Mine. I instantly decided not to respond to this email, which had no salutation, closing, or any punctuation. Clearly, the writer did need some form of "life coaching," whatever that was, but it wasn't going to come from me. I chose not to respond to her because of her lack of effort in establishing a connection.

This one's trickier:

Hello Ellis,

A past client of yours suggested I network with you. I have been working in various capacities as a general manager and as a management consultant for about 12 years. While I enjoy my work, several of my friends and colleagues have been aggressively urging me to move into the executive coaching field. While I have little training in this space, I have done quite a bit of it for a number of years through my consulting work and my professional network. If you have time and interest, I would like to speak with you about what brought you to Exec Coaching. Please let me know if you are interested and your availability for a telephone call.

Thank you,
Jesse Pinkman

Who is the "past client" who referred him? He doesn't even bother to mention the name, even though the best connection is direct referral. The phrase "suggested I network with you" shows a poor understanding of what real networking is. In this context, it sounds more like, "I want to exploit you," which is borne out by the rest of the email. "Several of my friends and colleagues have been aggressively urging me to move into the executive coaching field . . ." Wow. He's telling me that it wasn't his idea; other people came up with it, and he's doing it only because *they* suggested it? "I have little training in this space" is not exactly how you want to introduce yourself to anyone. Why point out your negatives in a first communication? Or any communication, for that matter. His interest in my background is entirely reasonable, but he closes his email by asking me to contact him, thereby putting the onus on me. He's already put the responsibility for his career choices on his friends, and now he's expecting me to follow-up with him, rather than the other way around. This made me think the situation was too complicated to tackle, and I didn't respond.

A private client was deep into interviews with one of the major investment banks, and he had been told by the hiring manager that he was the clear first choice. He was awaiting an offer. Instead, with no warning or even a hint, he received the following email:

Hi Jim,

Unfortunately, we already have a candidate with a better match for the position.

Al

Talk about branding! Aside from the devastating effect of this rather abrupt communication, this manager sent out a negative branding statement about himself and his company. What the manager didn't remember was that *his* manager had referred my client for the position. This kind of insensitive communication was not only hurtful to the recipient but also created political difficulty for the sender within his organization. (Remember, networking is everywhere.) There wasn't an explanation, not even a template rejection, even though my client had been told he was the lead candidate. What's left is a negative perception about an organization, about a professional in the organization. Not great business. Even a rejection letter should create a positive perception about the sender and the company.

As pointed out before, there's often a positive outcome to emails. (It's easier to focus on the bad ones, and I have many of them!) A current student sent the following email to me:

Ellis,

Thanks so much for taking the time out of your busy schedule to speak with me earlier this evening. As always, your advice and approach is spot on, and very well received on my end. I cannot thank you enough for all the guidance—hopefully this will all work out and we will celebrate in the months to come. I hope to see you around campus and look forward to keeping in touch. Thanks again.

David

Yes, it's nice to get praise for one's work but that's not why this is such a good communication. This student has been careful in all his communications with me throughout his work crisis; he's been sensitive to the fact that I have a complicated schedule, always acknowledging my accessibility despite those complications. He thinks about the other side of the desk and is appreciative, friendly, and direct. Most importantly, the email made me *want* to work with him, and he has made the process easier by his responsiveness and warmth. His skill at relationship building also made me confident that he'd be successful in pursuing a new career.

Here are a few pointers to help make your emails more effective:

- Respond in a timely manner. Even if you don't have time to fully respond, the brief acknowledgment of receipt ("I'll do my best to get back to you with more detail in a couple of days") assures the sender that the communication has been received.

- Proofread every email for grammar, punctuation, and tone before sending. This is a critical part of your personal branding.

- If you haven't been in touch with someone for a while, use a salutation and closing. Of course, if it's a back and forth within the same day, that's not necessary.

- Keep it short, simple, and direct. Great work-related communication shouldn't have long paragraphs or complex sentences. Get to the point so your email can be scanned fast.

- Check the recipient before hitting the "send" button. "Reply to all" has been a career killer for many. Slow down. The speed of the technology can be a detriment. I personally have made this error too many times.

Social Media

Here are a few facts that may seem startling: 46% of people search names of business associates or colleagues on the internet before meeting them; 93% of recruiters use search engines to learn about candidates; and 58% of recruiters report that they have eliminated candidates based on information they found online. I'd be willing to bet those numbers have increased by the time you read this chapter.

As with all the technology we've mentioned, there are new rules and new ways of thinking about controlling the perception you create. LinkedIn is probably the most critical tool in social media for people in business, and it's important to manage it well for both building new networks in the job search and building professional contacts.

Consider the template invitation, "I'd like to add you to my professional network." Think about it. Put yourself in the recipient's place. What is the message? To me, it's, "I'm sending you a form because I want to add you to my list, and I'm not really thinking about the person I'm writing to . . ." Or, "I just found your name on a list." Either way, it's impersonal, and it's not smart business or good branding for you. If you want to add someone to your LinkedIn database, why not make the message personal? Or if you don't know the person—maybe it's a level 3 distance from you— mention something or someone you have in common professionally and why you'd like to link up. It doesn't have to be a complicated communication, just some kind of personal acknowledgment. The template LinkedIn invitation reminds me of the impersonal holiday missives that detail everything everyone in the family has done in the past year. The "high touch" approach works a lot better, even if it's just one tailored sentence.

Today, I received one of those form invitations, so I checked to see who had sent it, even though my inclination would be to ignore impersonal invitations. I learned that the person was someone I liked and used to work with, so despite the impersonality, I did accept.

Would that template invitation be the brand you want to send out? Or is it worth taking a few seconds to personalize the message? Of course it is.

Here are a few suggestions for managing your LinkedIn profile:

- Stay on top of your profile and continuously update.

- Reach out to others and personalize your invitations (think customized, not generalized).

- Participate in groups. There are hundreds of professional, and college and graduate school affiliate groups—they offer a network that's almost as good as an alumni database.

Some professions, like advertising and media, use Facebook, Twitter, and other social media extensively. Here's where the mix of professional and personal blur and can lead to difficulty. If, for example, there are damaging and unfair commentaries that are easily searchable on Google, how can you control those? The following are suggestions to help you manage social media in general:

- Control how you are perceived. Start a blog, or engage in online discussions appropriate to your profession if you're concerned about damaging information.

- Search for yourself regularly, and consider using reputation management tools like Trackur, Google Alerts, Technorati, MonitorThis, and Naymz if there's a problem.

- Use Facebook's privacy controls (especially friend lists).

- If you don't want your family or boss to see it, keep it private.

- Restrict who can find your Facebook profile (via Facebook and Google).

- Be careful about your tone when you use social media (especially with Twitter because of its abbreviated length). Think about whether you'd like to hear those comments about you before writing them about someone else.

Conclusion

Thinking about yourself as an advertisement for your brand is imperative. I am not suggesting you're on stage all the time, but you are out there a good deal of your life, and it's important to try to manage how others see you. The person sitting next to you at a conference or in a social situation could be the person who refers you to the biggest deal of your life. But what if that person has seen you the day after Happy Hour, when you might not be making sense? Although socializing or partying are part of the work environment, do you want your colleagues, and others to see you that way week after week? Being human is entirely acceptable, but consistently branding yourself in a negative or insensitive way will not help your career.

Manage those perceptions and you will open up opportunities. Create the positive spin that will make everyone around you want to be one of those connections you are seeking in your career.

Chapter 5

Would You Please Remove Your Blouse?
The Five Interview Questions You Should Be Able to Answer

Frequently, job seekers worry about the long lists of possible interview questions out there and the books to match, like those with titles such as, *The Five Hundred Questions You* Absolutely *Need to Master for Your Next Interview!* Of course books with titles like that sell. Unfortunately, they only add to the anxiety that is already present, the last thing you need. If you actually read these books, you may get even more confused than when you started. Interviewing is tough enough. You're on the line. You're being judged. It's worse than dating. But good preparation can make all the difference. (I wish I could help with the dating issue as easily.)

I believe there are really only five questions you need to be able to answer. Preparing for those questions will enable you to go into the interview with more confidence.

I've presented this assertion to a wide range of clients and groups in nearly every conceivable profession over the past 25 years or so and have found that the five generic questions can be applied to almost any employment situation. I was challenged about this by the director of modeling for a leading "intimate apparel" (one of the great euphemisms) corporation many years ago. She said that she asked all of her job applicants a question that couldn't possibly fit into the five questions.

"Would you please remove your blouse?"

Definitely one of the most unusual questions I've ever heard and a great title for an article on this topic I wrote back then. By the end of our conversation, she saw it really was a basic content question and fit nicely into Question 3.

Question 1: Tell me about yourself (or the two-minute pitch)

This is the most common opening question, and, unfortunately, the most difficult. Variations may include, "Let's run through your resume" (asked by the pedantic interviewer), or "Why don't we review some of the major aspects of your career?" or "Could you give me a brief overview of your work background?" A 90-second to two-minute self-presentation module could make the difference between a successful job search and an ordinary, drawn-out meandering search. This presentation should be a well-organized—but not scripted—statement of skills, experience, and major strength areas and will set you apart from the majority of job seekers. Most interviewees will respond to such opening questions with a boring, and ultimately pointless, litany of jobs held since high school or college. Of course, an interviewer can easily find that information by looking at a resume, so why repeat what is already known? Think of your pitch as a well-crafted advertisement.

A pitch is also critical because most hiring decisions are made in the first five minutes of an interview. Ask people who do a lot of hiring. This doesn't mean you can't recover from a bad pitch, but a good one will set up the rest of the interview quite nicely. Think about what goes into those first five minutes. The pressure is on. Small talk. Great handshake. (The "dead fish" will kill any interview, so give up on all your grand career aspirations if you can't manage a good business handshake.) Good eye contact. And, "Tell me about yourself." If you find yourself in an interview where the question isn't asked, or the interviewer likes to talk a lot, make sure you get the pitch in, maybe by saying at some point, "Let me make this easy for you by giving you a thumbnail of my experience and skills."

A great pitch will also form the basis of most self-marketing activities in a job search, such as informational networking, phone screenings, unplanned meetings, social occasions, approach letters, ad responses, and follow-up letters. Ideally, the pitch should be prepared as an outline or a series of bullet points, which should make it easy to follow and clear for any audience. Assume that your listener(s) know little or nothing about you. Try to avoid lists, chronologies, and jargon. Too much detail is not likely to be assimilated, particularly at the beginning of a meeting.

I mentioned earlier that it's not a good idea to script as it can lead to some potential problems in pitching. A memorized speech will be perceived as both too crafted and often not targeted to the specific interview. When I spoke at the recruiters' meeting a few years ago, many corporate recruiters told me that applicants frequently sounded overly prepared, lacked conversational tone, and appeared almost robotic in their pitching. Practicing a pitch from an outline or bullet points should not only solve this problem but also enable you to adjust the pitch to the specific job or organization. Think of the pitch, along with the rest of the interview, as consultative selling. You're taking what the interviewer tells you, or what you've learned before the interview, and giving the interviewer what he/she needs to know.

To get you started, here is a suggested model for your two-minute pitch:

- **A label or positioning statement**

  What are you? How do you want people to see you? Make sure the listener can understand immediately what you are trying to say or what your goals are. If you can't label yourself precisely (maybe you're trying to change careers), your positioning statement will describe a combination of roles.

- **Two or three experience/skill areas**

  What do you want to highlight? These may change from situation to situation. Expand on one of these with concrete evidence (maybe three sentences). What was a significant accomplishment in your career that you want to emphasize for this listener? What are you most proud of that will show you off to best advantage?

- **A unique selling proposition**

  What makes you different from your competition? Show that your combination of skills and experiences add up to a professional who has something different to offer. This is probably the toughest part of a pitch. "Unique" may be a bit of an overstatement —something tough to achieve. You want to make clear why you should be seen as different from the majority of applicants.

- **Settings or branding**

  Where have you worked? Figure out if naming the places will help you, pigeonhole you, or confuse the listener. Sometimes "leading financial services institution" works better than "JP Morgan Chase," depending on your target. Sometimes, the listener will not know the name of the company you worked for, say, in the dotcom era, so mentioning the function will work better. You may want to combine the two —perhaps the name of the brand name company along with the dotcom function.

- **Summarize**

  You should create a synopsis of all that you have said so far. Make sure the listener not only has heard the points stated above but also hears them in a different way. This is pure self-marketing—your personal advertisement.

Sometimes, you might have a highly marketable skill but don't want to continue featuring it as a major part of your professional presentation. In this situation, it is a delicate operation to effectively balance the two considerations. You may end up dropping the highly marketable skill because you just don't want to be perceived in that way.

Question 2: Why are you looking for a job? Why did you leave your last one?

This is frequently too personal and complex an issue to be addressed in a general way. There are too many variations to cover in a short chapter. However, a few points should be stated. You should not volunteer or overstate information that could be negatively construed. Don't offer information like, "I left the company because I didn't like the way the company was run and wanted to be proactive," or "I was bored and wanted a new challenge." Those answers could create the perception that perhaps you were the problem, not the company; something you definitely want to avoid. It's fine to offer some explanation but only when asked. If you bring it up, it sounds like you might have something to hide.

But you do need what I like to call your "rationale." In the case of a downsizing, organizational layoff, restructuring, or merger, be sure to point out you were part of a group of people being let go. This is the easiest explanation for a potential employer to understand. You hold no real grudge against the company for it; and you were only somewhat disappointed because it had been a great experience due to your opportunities for . . . (fill in the skills and experiences right now!). Here's where you can turn this issue into a series of selling points.

Whenever possible, indicate it was your decision to leave—even though you might have been asked to leave. It's important to understand that losing a job is not a career killer, contrary to the popular mythology. Many of my clients have difficulty getting past that and see themselves as damaged goods. It's now generally understood people lose jobs more than once in their working lives and are not adversely affected in their ability to find a new job—except when the job seeker has trouble with a rationale for having left the job or feels somehow there's a stigma.

I strongly recommend you adhere to one of the main rules of self-marketing: never speak ill of your former employer(s) or any previous work situations. This is not only a basic tenet of sales and marketing but also an imperative in presenting yourself positively. Speaking negatively about any other work situations creates the perception that you're a malcontent. Not exactly the perception you want to create.

Also remember, you never left a job for "more of a challenge." That implies to a prospective employer you'd leave them, too, the first time you get bored or feel underpaid. Instead, you're seeking to put together a combination of skills from several settings, your education, and interests, and you aren't able to see a path where you could move forward at your current job. You want to utilize what you know. Always make it clear the next step is a logical one, not because your last boss threw something at you, or there were ethically questionable activities going on around you, or you didn't like the people you worked with. The move should seem as if it is part of your overall plan, even though it may not be. Keep in mind that interviewing, like all other aspects of job search, is marketing, and creating the right perception is just as important as possessing the right skill set.

Question 3: Why should we hire you?

I hope no one is quite so abrasive as to phrase this kind of question in that way, but it is the gist of most interview questions. These kinds of questions are the content questions, the bulk of any interview, the questions that ask about your skills and experiences.

"What are your strengths?" "What did you do best at your last position?" "What gave you the most difficulty?" "How well do you adapt to rapidly changing technologies?" "Do you know how to . . .?" "Have you had experience in . . .?" "What kind of management style works best for you?" And, of course, the dumbest interview question, "What are your weaknesses?" (But more about that one later.)

This is when you get to show what you know and prove to the interviewer that you are the best candidate for the job. Your goal should be to attempt to turn questions into "war stories," which will clearly illustrate your successes.

Part of the preparation for interviews is setting up your war stories. In some of the organizations where I've worked, they call them "PARs" (Problem/Action/Result), "CARs" (Context/Action/Result), or in one unfortunate consulting firm, "SARs" (Situation/Action/Result), until the disease with that acronym appeared on the international scene, and they were compelled to change many of their printed materials.

You should prepare at least five or six of these war stories before every interview, perhaps adapting some of the bullets off your resume. But you need to make sure the stories match what you think the organization is going to want from you. Don't just walk into the interview with a generic batch of examples, assuming they'll work in every situation. As with the two-minute pitch, you should not script these stories. You want your interview to sound like a conversation.

A good interview should include at least two or three of your war stories. The key to getting those into the interview is how well you perfect "the art of the segue." That is, for all you non-musicians, how well you work your stories into the conversation by directly connecting them with a question asked. For example, if an interviewer asks you to talk about a specific skill, you wouldn't answer with "Yes, I am very organized." That would end a conversation fast, and then the interviewer would have to come up with another question, and the interview might take on an awkward tone.

The better answer is, "Yes, I'm quite comfortable with organizing complex assignments. *For example*, when I was working at ABC Corp, we were working on . . ." and then you're off and running into a nice two- or three-minute war story. The advantages of being prepared with war stories are that you get to illustrate the skill they're seeking, and you take charge of the interview. It's important to realize most interviewers are not very good at interviewing and would prefer if you offer information that will make their jobs easier—in both the interviewing sense and in the sense that you're going to fill their requirements. They don't want to have to drill for information. What you want is for the interviewer to not only walk away from the interview with the impression that you're an interesting, energetic, charming, and smart person but also someone who has demonstrated skill and experience in the key areas of the job. With the war story response, you have presented concrete examples, not just broad generalizations.

But what about those negative questions? It's important to remember what self-marketing is all about. Try to stick to this proposition: your career has been sunshine, light, and success. There are no negatives. Negatives raise problems. You have no problems. So what do you do when you'll inevitably get that silly, "What are your weaknesses?" question?

I call the question silly because it's a no-win for the person who's being interviewed. It's a trap question. In most circumstances, it doesn't really show the interviewer much; it's the sign of an inexperienced or poorly prepared interviewer who can't think of good skills-based questions. If you stick to the concept that there are no negatives, then you're not going to directly answer the question. Many interviewees have reported to me they feel obligated to "tell the truth, the whole truth, and nothing but the truth." I never encourage anyone to lie on an interview (it doesn't usually work), but I certainly don't think you should answer all questions with full, unfiltered responses.

The best response to the weakness question is to have a couple of prepared war stories ready, which illustrate how you turned around a negative—five years ago. You want some distance from that negative. For example, maybe you had some difficulty learning how to delegate when you had your first management position. A great way to answer the weakness question is to illustrate how you overcame that issue, and how you have subsequently turned what you learned into a strength. Use that strategy as much as possible with other negative questions as well. If you can't think fast enough, some stonewalling will suffice. For example, "I can't think of anything right now. Although I have shortcomings, as most people do, nothing major has been pointed out to me in this regard so far in my career. My appraisals have been very good." Stay away from the "too good to be true" statements like, "My coworkers think I take my work too seriously." No one ever believes those.

Question 4: Where do you see yourself in five years?

This one is almost as pointless as the weakness/negative question. But it's asked frequently. A time filler. Sometimes, it's okay for recent college graduates (they might not have a lot to talk about) but not for experienced professionals. Consider the real subtext of the question, which is that most interviewers are not particularly interested in applicants' overall career plans, unless they're about to make a job offer and are really asking, "If offered this position, will you stay committed to us and to your field of interest? Or are you using this as a stepping stone to something else?" Of course, most of us don't really plan our careers so concretely, or sometimes, we really *are* using the job as a bridge job or a stepping stone to something else. But we certainly don't want to say that.

It would be best to answer these, "Just what do you want to be when you grow up?" questions with a plan for future growth within the same discipline (not what your promotion ambitions are), demonstrating a strong enthusiasm for what you do and your commitment to it. Organizations like to hire employees who are excited about what they do. Indicate this is all part of a plan that has been evolving throughout your career, even if you're transitioning between toll collector and nuclear physics. There's always a connection between all you've done, and you want to describe that. Part of this could be lifted straight from your two-minute pitch, which is your statement of how you want to market yourself. Of course, this response needs to be prepared in advance of the interview. Even when applicants are making radical career changes (like the toll collector), it is always possible to demonstrate consistent themes in one's career.

Question 5: How much did you earn at your last job? What are you looking for in this one?

Negotiations start the second an interviewer or screener asks about money, long before an interview might take place. This could even be a human resources phone screen. The most important thing to know is that in this, the first step of salary negotiation, you want to try to avoid the issue. However, there are two types of interviewers who will not let you get away with this—recruiters and human resources professionals. That's what they're paid to do, which is to screen you out and prepackage the compensation issues prior to interviews with the decision makers.

This is why you want to avoid human resources and recruiters in an effective job search. Yes, it's true it's easier to get a job this way. They do all the work, refer you to the right place (if there's a fit somewhere), and you're all packaged and ready to go. Unfortunately, the current employment statistics all show that getting jobs through recruiters and direct human resources contacts is roughly somewhere around a 5–6% probability. I would never say job searchers should not utilize these resources, but they certainly shouldn't depend on them or spend much energy trying to get a new job that way. Pay attention to those statistics! Avoiding those resources will enable you to negotiate more effectively.

I'll discuss the art of salary negotiations in greater detail in Chapter 6. But let me just say briefly that if you're able to defer money conversations, your worth will increase as you have more time to build value. There are two points to consider: the person who gives dollar figures first usually loses out in the long run, and the longer the conversations go on without discussing money, the higher the price goes.

It's not always possible to defer salary discussions. But you should try. One possible way would be to say, "I hate to rule myself out because of a too-high or too-low figure. Certainly, I want to be paid well, but right now the fit is my key issue. So, if it's okay with you, could we defer the conversation until later on when we've figured out if it's a good fit?" And, if that doesn't work well, you might want to try, "Could you give me an idea of what your range is?" Or, "I'm sure we'll be able to work something out, if your company's salary structure is within the usual market levels." Be aware of the interviewer's reactions to your attempts. If you sense annoyance, after a couple of tries, give a wide salary range.

An overall strategy of interviewing would be—to paraphrase President Kennedy—ask not what the employer can do for you but what you can do for the employer. Or, perhaps, think like a consultant, which is to figure out what it is that the employer seeks and fit your responses to his or her needs. This will help you focus on what I think is the key, namely marketing yourself directly to the potential employer. Evaluating a possible offer, sizing up the organization, or contemplating career growth only clouds the main issue, which is to build the prospective employer's interest and get asked back for the next round. I frequently advise my clients to defer all of their self-interest issues until after the point of offer. Without extraneous thoughts, it's far easier to concentrate on the major task—getting the offer.

Preparing the five questions carefully for the interview, along with thoroughly researching the organization, will significantly reduce the stress that almost everyone feels in an interview (including the interviewer) and will help you avoid surprises. A surprise question, for example, might have been the "Please remove your blouse" request that I mentioned earlier. It fits perfectly into #3 or the "CAR" category because the answer would provide evidence to the interviewer that the candidate can do the job. In this case, it's an unusual, visual war story, but it is the evidence that the interviewer was seeking.

Chapter 6

Don't Leave Money on the Table

Back in the 1980s, I was struggling with a very difficult job search. The kind where you wake up in the middle of the night, every night, imagining you're never going to find a job, are completely unemployable, and will end up living in a cardboard box in Central Park.

I was attempting a transition from a traditional large corporate setting to a consulting firm; I was getting great meetings . . . and no offers. My conclusions were the kind most job seekers come to when they're in this state of complete self-absorption: I had "too much traditional corporate experience and didn't understand the consulting environment" or was "too young" or "didn't look the part" or a variety of other (mostly ridiculous) explanations. I knew my field pretty well and knew how to do a decent search but was ultimately too impatient. I wanted immediate results. It was, overall, a humbling experience, trying to do what I was supposed to be helping others to do. And, as I found out later, it was a great learning experience when it came to the negotiating part.

Finally, an offer. The awful search was over. I was so excited that I almost announced to the president of the consulting firm, "I'll start in an hour!" Actually, I contained myself and did something even worse—I negotiated the offer on the spot. In my desperation to finally end the ordeal, I violated one of the most important rules of negotiating: I didn't listen to the advice I had already given so many others. Turned out the offer was somewhat less than my previous salary, so I asked for an amount that would at least make the new salary a lateral move. The offer was immediately increased to meet my request; I agreed to accept. I asked about the benefits plan and was told it was "the usual." That sounded good to me! Ordeal over.

Unfortunately, "the usual" was not so great. There was a six-month wait for coverage, which ended up costing me the entire difference between the original offer and what I had "negotiated." Not only that, but I never asked about reviews, 401K, 401K matches, bonuses, career path, vacation, and more. The shoemaker had botched his own shoes.

I have heard about every imaginable salary negotiation scenario—internal and external—through my private practice, students at Columbia Business School and New York University, clients at various job search organizations, and presentations I've made.

Here is what I think are the three critical points of a salary negotiation:

1. Avoiding the subject

First, *try to avoid the subject for as long as you can.* Of course, you will be well prepared when you go into the offer phase because you'll have carefully researched appropriate compensation levels either via salary surveys or through your personal network. There are four reasons why you don't want to talk about money too early in an interviewing process:

- If you mention a salary the hiring manager thinks is too low for someone at your level, you might be creating the perception that you're not as good as you say you are.

- If you mention a low salary or low salary expectations, a hiring manager might think she could be a hero to the company and bring you in at a level that is lower than where you should be. Save the company some money, right? This is bad hiring policy because when an employee finds out the compensation is less than people are making at the same level or skill set, there will be resentment and probable turnover.

- If you mention a high salary or high salary expectations that place you outside the hiring manager's range, it could easily eliminate you from consideration. You might be thinking, "Why do I even want to consider this process if their salary is going to be lower than what I used to make?" Wrong thinking. This is 2013. We shouldn't be thinking about only a salary figure anymore. According to most surveys, standard benefit packages are usually worth about 30–35% or more of the salary. So add that on while figuring this out. And what about those 401Ks, 403Bs, and matching from the employer? And bonus and equity—maybe even pension—when those are in the mix? We always need to think about "total comp" rather than an absolute salary number. That's been one of the major changes over the past several years in how we should think about compensation.

- If you happen to be in exactly the right range, you've limited your opportunity of negotiating more when the offer comes. What if the position requires more than you expected? What if you dazzle the hiring manager with your wit, charm, and brilliance, and the position becomes more significant and complex? You're still stuck with the numbers you mentioned too early in the process.

If you manage to avoid the topic of money early on, chances are you will have more opportunity to build value and increase your negotiating abilities when there is an offer. The hiring manager will have a clearer picture of your true worth. Your objective is to avoid being screened out because of a number and continue the process of selling and demonstrating a great fit so that the number increases the longer the process goes on.

Now comes the tricky part. How do you avoid discussing the subject when the interviewer asks you within, perhaps, the first ten minutes of the first interview what you were earning on the last job, or what you're "looking for"?

You can't say, "I'd rather talk about this later." Some of the people I've met over the years internalize the idea that avoiding the subject is always good, and then they feel free to tell the interviewer they'd rather not talk about it. Not a good relationship builder!

You can say, "I'd hate to eliminate myself because of a dollar figure at this point. Right now, the key issue for me is finding a great fit. I figure if the fit is there, then we'll work out the money part. **If it's okay with you**, could we talk about this a little later on in the process?" This frequently works. But, sometimes it doesn't.

What if the interviewer comes right back with, "That's very nice and all, but I need to know what your last salary was. I don't want to waste my time . . . or yours."

Turning the question around with, "Could you give me an idea of your range?" often works. If the range is anywhere close to where you think you should be, you can say, "Oh, we'll be able to work this out easily." If it's way below your range, then you might want to indicate that by saying, "It's a little lower than what my current expectations are, but I'd like to continue our conversation. It's not always strictly about the money for me." You want to keep the conversation going, unless the numbers are so ridiculously low you know there's no chance you'll be able to "work this out."

What if the hiring manager starts to get a little irritated? "Okay, I understand that you don't want to talk about it, but I really need to know."

No matter what the original question was, you might respond with, "I'll be looking for a total compensation package in the range of . . ." If that doesn't work, it's time to give in.

A few notes about "giving in." Never fabricate a previous salary number. A prospective employer can always ask for a W-2 on the first day of employment; if it's discovered that you've invented the numbers, you're gone. Many companies do that. If you want to make your previous salary seem larger, you might want to say, "My *total* compensation was in the range of . . ." and you'll be including all those benefits, bonuses, etc. Conversely, if you want to keep it low because you're seeking the right job more than the money at this moment, you can say, "My base was . . ." If you're moving from one field to another, or from a commission-based job to a salaried one, you might want to bring in the apples and oranges comparison, indicating that it's tough to compare the two because of the differences in the way people are compensated. Or, if your total compensation varied enormously over a five-year period, you could say, "In the very good years, my numbers were as high as . . ." and "When the company was having some difficulty, the numbers were lower." You'd adjust that to whether or not you want the appearance of having had high or low compensation.

I wish I could say these techniques work all of the time. But I can promise they work more often than not and are definitely worth your effort. Trying to avoid the money discussion in initial stages of interviewing is a key aspect of successful negotiating. The minute someone mentions money, even before the first interview on a screening call, a negotiation process has begun. Try not to fall into the traps.

Where does an avoidance technique usually *not* work? That's easy—with recruiters and human resources professionals. Their job is to screen out, not to necessarily screen in, and salary is a key part of the screening process. Since I strongly urge clients to focus primarily on directly contacting hiring managers in their search, human resources professionals and recruiters should generally be a small segment of a search.

2. Defer the real negotiation

The second critical point of salary negotiation is, *Don't negotiate at the point of offer.* Nearly all offers are somewhat negotiable. In trying to think of situations where they're not, Wall Street law firms, entry-level investment bank positions, civil service, and a few others come to mind. But even in those situations, there might be some leeway. Most people who hire have some "play money"; they usually go to the offer with some idea of how much more they can give if the applicant wants to negotiate. It's understood there will be negotiation.

Many of the people I've met have felt uncomfortable even thinking about this subject. They're so grateful and happy about an offer, they accept on the spot. That usually means leaving money on the table. And always, after employment begins, they're thinking there could have been, should have been, more.

Others will feel that, as a result of all the rejection inherent in any job search, they should take the offer immediately because it might be rescinded. In this process, people tend to feel skeptical, with good reason. All those false starts, all those cancelled appointments, all those, "You're our lead candidate" promises have come and gone, so why believe this offer will withstand a few more days?

I remember a client from several years ago who received a good offer after a long and painful search. He replied to the offer by expressing his excitement at the prospect of such a good job and asked for two or three days to "think about some of the questions and details we haven't covered" so that they could tie up all the loose ends and close the deal. The prospective employer was clearly annoyed with this request. She said she didn't understand why he needed any time at all but would give him until the end of the day.

I told him there might be something wrong with the position or company since it was highly unusual for an employer to demand such a quick turnaround response. I said he did need time to do a little research and plan his strategy. He called the employer back that afternoon, and she rescinded the offer, stating that she didn't want to hire someone who "waffled." This, after a two-month interviewing process! After he threatened me with some fairly extreme violence, I convinced him to look into the situation further. He found out the next day that there had been seven people in his position in the previous year! I have heard several versions of this story from other clients as well. When an offer is rescinded, there is usually something very wrong with the situation.

What to do, then, when the offer is actually extended? Something very important happens at this point; the balance of power has shifted. Before the offer, you're the person on the other side of the desk, trying to convince someone you are the right person for the job. After the offer, it is now established that you *are* the person for the job. The hiring manager does not want to settle for Number Two or Number Three; he wants you.

Here are three scenarios:

- The offer is too low. Your response should be silence. You're taking it in, thinking about it, counting to 10. This may put the person who's making the offer on the defensive, and in many instances, there is a possibility of an immediate increase to the offer. Sometimes, that person might ask if there's a problem, because the silence might create some discomfort. That's a good thing! Whether or not there is a response to the silence, your next statement should be something like, "I'm very excited about the possibility of joining the company. I think we'd work together well. The department seems well positioned to (fill in the blank). The offer seems a little low for what I think my market is, but I'd like a few days to think it over. Could we make a plan to get together then? I think we'll be able to work things out at that point."

What's happened with this response is that you've bought time to work out a strategy—and planted the idea that there might be a problem with the package offered. Try hard to avoid negotiating on the telephone, whenever possible. It's much better to do it face-to-face on a more equal footing. The telephone puts you at a disadvantage; you can't read body language or facial expressions.

- The offer is somewhere in the range you expected. The response should be almost the same as in the first scenario—silence and then a request for time. The only difference would be that there would be no suggestion that the compensation is too low.

- The offer is terrific. You're trying to calm yourself in order to maintain a businesslike demeanor, but you want to say, "Yes! Yes! Yes!" You don't. No silence this time. All you have to say is that you don't think there'll be any problem with the compensation, but you'd like time to think over the details, and perhaps will have some questions to clarify. ("Clarify" is one of my favorite negotiation words.)

What's been accomplished by deferring a real negotiating session is that you will be able to take in all the facts of the offer and work out a clear strategy.

3. Plan an "Everyone Wins" strategy

An "Everyone Wins" strategy is the third and final critical point of salary negotiation. A good negotiating meeting is not a contest. It should have a collegial tone. The word "we" is preferable to the word "I." It's not a matter of "I need," it's an issue of "Could we?"

In planning a negotiating strategy, you get to list everything you've wanted to ask all along. Not just about the money or the benefits or the bonuses but details about job responsibilities, reporting relationships —everything. Now that the balance of power has shifted, you can ask all those self-interest questions you've been avoiding to this point. (After all, the interview process is about what you can do for *them*; now it's time for what they can do for *you*.)

Of course, there are enormous variations of tone in this process, as there are in all of the other phases of negotiating. For example, an equities trader might be more direct than a brand manager or a creative director, depending on the culture. But no matter what field you're in, you need to plan your strategy around a prioritized list. Make sure the first and maybe the second are easy questions; questions you don't care about that much but will ease both sides into the negotiation. For example, you might want to ask about when you can get into the company 401K. That is never negotiable because it's predetermined by a set of federal regulations. You don't want to get to the hardcore issues right away because that's what the hiring manager expects . . . and because you want to set up a positive tone of cooperation.

Decide what's important to you, prioritize, then mix in your major issues (vacation, bonus, car allowance, equity, quality of life) with the items that don't matter as much to you. Maybe #1 and #2 are not important, #3 is about bonus structure, #4 is about a particular reporting relationship, #5 is about annual reviews, and #6 is another relatively unimportant item. Be prepared to lose some and win some, which should produce the desired win/win overall. Decide before you go into this round of negotiating what your "drop dead" total compensation number is. By "drop dead," I don't mean that should be your response to the hiring manager if the offer doesn't comply with your wishes. What I mean is that you have decided beforehand what the bottom is and won't go below it. You don't want to end up compromising so much that you take a job where you will be unhappy and resentful. I tell my clients that if they settle too much, I look forward to seeing them again next year when they begin their next search.

What about the money? If that's your first key issue, then you pose it, perhaps, like this: "The dollar figure you offered is lower than what I've determined my market to be. How can **we** get it higher?" The manager might respond by asking what you consider a fair figure. And you'll suggest a number above what you will accept. You may even want to cite some of your research sources. The manager will probably suggest another meeting to discuss this further and want to go over other points on the list. Or the manager might state there's little room for movement on the salary number. You could, later on, suggest there might be other methods to think about, such as a signing bonus, two consecutive six-month reviews, and clearly stated benchmarks for clearly defined increases. The selling that was an emphasis in the interviewing process should continue. Remind the hiring manager of why the number should be higher, based on what you've accomplished and your consistently demonstrated skills. Selling doesn't really stop until the negotiation is complete.

This part of negotiating might be a back and forth, much like a conflict resolution process. Keep it level, stick to the facts, and suggest alternatives. No emotions allowed. Don't give in quickly, especially if you're feeling pressured to end the process. This might take a few separate conversations.

What about the vacations? Some organizations will not recognize seniority—officially. I know of one client whose vacation time was more important to him than the compensation. The company had a policy of two weeks to start, when the client had already earned four weeks a year for several years. (Note the word "earned"; it's a good word to use here.) The company seemed intransigent on the issue. My client suggested the company increase his salary base by two weeks (or $2/52^{nds}$ of an annual salary). He could then take off two weeks a year in addition to the two weeks already granted by policy without pay. The hiring manager agreed. In other instances, I've heard that managers will suggest "mental health" days as a tacit agreement.

Sometimes, the agreements will not be put in writing. For example, discretionary bonuses are rarely specified in an offer letter. But if the bonus is based on benchmarks, it should be in writing. You should always ask about what those discretionary criteria are, even if they can't be put in your offer letter.

And, finally, what about the issue of severance? I say "finally" here because it should be the last issue discussed. You certainly don't want to bring up severance as a primary issue and give the impression that you think things are going to go wrong. But you do want protection. Ask the hiring manager what happens in the case of a takeover, a merger, or a change in the direction of the business. What "protection" do you have in that event? At more senior levels, this can evolve into a major piece of the negotiation. At middle management or professional levels, it may be strictly a matter of organizational policy. Or it might be another "drop dead" issue.

Recently, I worked with a client on negotiations that included relocation, and she had decided that the severance agreement could make or break the whole deal, not wanting to be stuck in a new city with no protection. She was able to work out a satisfactory compromise on that basis.

Although the variations in negotiating strategies can vary widely, using the three strategies should improve the outcome of most compensation discussions. Many think negotiating a job package is strictly for senior people in an organization or for people who are unusually assertive. I have met so many people over the past years who are startled to find that they, too, can improve significantly on the original offer. I am always surprised when someone tells me it's not in their "nature" to try. Nothing to lose, plenty to gain. Basic salary negotiating is essentially a no-lose proposition. More of a "Why not?" than an "I can't." I have found these strategies work with a broad spectrum of job seekers—all levels, all kinds of positions, and all fields.

So go for it!

Chapter 7

Ads and Recruiters: Hard to Ignore, But . . .

I've been arguing with myself about this chapter since starting the book. The argument has been whether or not to include this subject. I believe that relying on recruiters and ads is not a good primary search methodology, frequently overvalued as a resource. However, they cannot be ignored. Fortunately, there are some techniques you can use that will help these methods work better, which I will discuss later in this chapter. But first let me tell you a little about why I think you should include these methods as a small part of your search.

Most job searchers immediately start by looking at ads or calling recruiters and hope they can succeed quickly with this reactive technique. Sounds good, doesn't it? Except that it doesn't work very well. The numbers speak loudly. Every year or so, I investigate how well the various search techniques function, and usually the ads and recruiters together, according to the research, account for around 12–13% of the overall job market. The more professional or senior the job, the less market penetration for ads and recruiters (except, sometimes, at the very high levels or for very technical or narrow scope positions). Most jobs, as we've discussed in other sections of the book, are found through personal networks. The problem is that in depending on ads and recruiters, many job seekers don't focus enough on what actually has a far better chance of success. They'll focus on a technique that involves a disproportionate amount of rejection, which fuels negativism in a search. So, why do people depend so much on the 13% and not the 87%?

That's easy. The other techniques, involving contact development, are more difficult. Spending hours and hours researching companies and targets and building networks piece by piece, often without the immediate gratification of interviews and then offers, is frustrating and complicated. One of the toughest parts of career transition in general is the lack of continuous feedback and quick results. The prospect of answering an ad, for example, and then getting called for an interview sounds easier and more appealing because it *is* easier.

Why don't ads and recruiters account for more jobs? Because most people do not precisely fit into the specific skill sets recruiters and ads are primarily seeking. If you're one of those professionals who has been doing the same basic job for your entire career and are seeking to move upward, you'll have a better shot with ads and recruiters. Or, more likely, you're one of the vast majority of applicants who doesn't precisely fit the job description. You may be perfectly *qualified* for the job, but if your resume isn't exactly what's being asked for, point by point, you'll be disqualified on that basis rather than on your overall credentials. For example, if a recruiter is seeking someone who has been working for a Big Four accounting firm in general audit for seven years with a set of specific skills, and you fit those skills perfectly except for the Big Four experience, your chances are not good for getting the interview. Of course, this is probably unfair and doesn't necessarily make sense but that's how most ads and recruiters function. They've been given a spec list by a hiring manager or a human resources recruiter, and their primary function is to find resumes that match it perfectly. They're deluged with huge numbers of resumes to sort through. Chances are most applicants will not fit the spec list.

Ads

When I recruited for a large bank many years ago, I used ads in *The New York Times* for large projects and occasionally for hard-to-fill positions. In one instance, we were opening a large data center and were staffing it at all levels. There were 36 positions for which we advertised internally as well as in *The Times*. It was a half-page ad, a major and expensive recruiting effort, and we received 5,000 responses for the 36 positions within two days. We were only a staff of four and had to figure out a way to get the best possible candidates for the positions as quickly as the hiring managers had requested, after having filled maybe five of the jobs from internal candidates.

5000 resumes! We split up the jobs and split up the resumes, 1250 per staff person. Our goal was to get five candidates to interview for each position. I cannot speak for all corporate recruiters, but I can say that what followed was fairly typical of many I've met over the years. I had responsibility for seven of the positions and actually ended up reading maybe 250 of my 1250 resumes in order to find enough initial candidates for each position. Basically this means 1000, or 80%, of the resumes were never even read on this first pass. Later on, I might have read an additional 100 if I'd been unable to find enough qualified candidates for a specific position or two.

You have probably had the experience at some point of reading the perfect ad practically screaming, "This job's for you!" And you write a great cover letter to accompany your brilliant resume that fits the job perfectly. And you send it to someone like . . . me, at the big corporation, the guy who only needs to read roughly 20% of the resumes he receives. In other words, there's a high probability that yours will never receive so much as a glance.

You end up feeling terrible because either you get a form rejection letter (from the better companies who are conscious of their public perception) or nothing (from the organizations who don't think that way). You may also end up feeling that something was wrong with your resume, cover letter, or credentials, when in fact that was not the case. This is only one reason, among many, why answering ads is essentially a crap shoot. But in a comprehensive job search, it's a technique not to be ignored because even in a gamble, there's a chance for success.

Ironically, the staffing professionals are often the ones who do the advertising and screening themselves prior to the actual hiring manager meeting the candidate. Clearly there is a disconnect in this process, another reason why building networks to decision makers is a far more effective search technique. You don't want to present your credentials to people whose purpose is to screen out. You'd rather present to the decision makers themselves. Ads are also highly competitive. Wouldn't you rather be one of three people being considered and not one of, say, 300?

A great technique for utilizing ads is to see them as information resources. For example, you see one that advertises for a position that interests you. Answer the ad, but also figure out a way to network into the company via a personal contact or perhaps through LinkedIn. Get referred directly. If you get to someone who's not in the department, mention you had heard "through the grapevine" there might be an opening in the XYZ area of the organization, and you were asking for advice on how you should proceed other than answering the ad. You might get a personal introduction. Or, if you're fortunate enough to locate the actual department and obtain an informational/networking meeting, you wouldn't even mention the ad or the "grapevine." Just present yourself as a perfect match to a job you supposedly don't even know about. Sneaky, but effective.

Ads are also an information source about what your possible markets might be. Even just perusing professional journals, online sites, and local papers might get you some ideas of where potential openings may be. This bit of research may also give you some new ideas about other options.

Ad response emails/letters are pretty direct. But what if you see a "perfect" job but realize that one or two things they're asking for are missing from your resume? Here's where I suggest a resume cover email/letter. Say that you have just started your search but have not completed a resume. However, you were excited about the position advertised and wanted to respond quickly. Instead of a resume, you list the items in the ad—but only the ones you fit—and then describe your proficiency in the second corresponding column. In other words, you're leaving out what you don't have and focusing on what you do offer. This is a tailored approach that emphasizes what you *can* do for the organization, bypassing some minor credential that you don't have and doesn't matter in your estimation.

Answer the ad twice. First, answer it immediately, and then . . . answer it again, maybe 10 days later. The second response will be received in a batch of maybe three, rather than the hundreds elicited earlier. Even in a small organization, an ad will draw many responses, even if only placed in a specialized trade publication. Don't worry that someone will notice the two responses. First of all, it would be surprising to me if someone would actually notice a duplicate, and, even if that were the case, so what? Would it be perceived as a negative if two responses were noted? Does it appear desperate? My take would be that the candidate was extremely interested in the position. What could be wrong with that?

Recruiters

Employment agencies, executive search, contingency, retainer, headhunter. Whatever the euphemism or professional distinction, all of these are different versions of recruiters. In this section, I will be talking about external recruiters (for example, those who are paid by organizations to find candidates to fill positions). Internal recruiters are those who work for the organizations themselves and are usually housed in human resources departments.

Contingency recruiters are paid only if they make the placement. Usually, contingency recruiters are tapped for lower to upper mid-level positions, but there is overlap. Many organizations will let several contingency recruiters know about an open position, so the competition will be fierce. Retained recruiters have an exclusive to fill a position and usually receive an upfront fee with the balance for completion of the assignment. Often, a retainer assignment is for a more senior role in an organization, although if the recruiting firm has a specific type of arrangement with the firm, it may be for several positions at different levels. The retained search is often slower and more thorough (no competition issue); some of the top-tier recruiting firms will have a research staff that fully vets candidates before presentation to employers.

Every now and then, I hear about a recruiter asking for an upfront fee from an applicant. This used to be an occasional practice, many years ago, but is never done by reputable firms now. Don't work with someone who asks for money. The fee should always be paid by the company that's hiring.

Probably the best resource for listings of search firms is *The Directory of Executive and Professional Recruiters* by Kennedy Career Services. I've found it's more effective to use the directory manually rather than by its online or CD versions. A rolling mailing to roughly five or six per week seems a good way to get the resume out there in recruiter land, for maybe five to six weeks, just to test that market. Don't be discouraged if you get only one or two form postcards, form email responses, or even nothing. Sometimes a positive response will come later on. This is very much like answering ads—a crap shoot.

The best way to connect to recruiters is to be referred by your personal network. But, even then, it's still not a great search technique. Remember those numbers mentioned earlier: perhaps 6–7% of jobs are filled this way.

Not to cast aspersions on an entire profession, but you must keep one thing in mind when dealing with recruiters.

Acting as your agent to get you a job is not their main purpose. Their priorities are as follows: (1) the organizational client's need (you know, those who pay the bill); (2) their personal income; and (3) you. Remember that order. Their purpose is to fill a position in the way that the corporate client requests, and then . . . to make the sale. This is not necessarily in your best interest.

What does a recruiter want to see when you meet? I think it's important to have a live meeting whenever possible. After all, this person is representing you, and it's your career we're talking about. Serious business. The recruiters who see their function as pushing paper are not the ones you want representing you.

Several years ago, I was advising a client who had been the CEO of a small financial services firm. He came to my office one day and told me he wanted to prepare for an interview with one of the Big Four executive search firms for a major opportunity. I asked him if he had enough time to go home and change for the interview because he was wearing a tee shirt and jeans. He said that was ridiculous because it was "only" a meeting with a recruiter. Wrong. The main reason the headhunter wanted to meet him was to see how well he presented so he'd feel comfortable referring my client to the corporate client. My client thought his skills, experience, and credentials were all that mattered. Yes, those are important, but image is also critical.

Treat this kind of interview exactly as you would any interview. You should not only dress appropriately but also don't allow the relationship to become too friendly and casual. That's a way for the recruiter to find out any negative material in your history, and, of course, there *is* no negative material. You answer questions as you would on any interview; there should be no difference in approach.

Many years ago, I had the strange experience of going to a group interview. I hadn't known in advance it would be a group since I had responded to an ad. An external recruiter conducted the interview. He took the entire day to get the large group of candidates weeded out until there were five still standing. It was grueling, with a long Q&A with the recruiter, then a written essay and a questionnaire. Come to think of it, it sounds now like the equivalent of some dopey reality TV show.

I didn't get voted off the island and somehow ended up one of the five finalists. (I've never been able to figure this out, since I was really not a good candidate for this position.) We were invited back a second day for psychological testing and an interview by a psychologist hired by the company. Already, I felt somewhat suspicious of this peculiar hiring process. And it was exhausting. I did the testing, a type of Myers-Briggs rip-off that was easy to manipulate for someone who knew this testing as I did, and then after hours of this, the psychological interview followed. This is where my big stumble occurred. Since then, I have always been aware that I should never let my guard down. After about an hour and a half of the interview, the psychologist asked me if I had any weaknesses in the work environment, a typical tricky interview question. I flippantly said I didn't particularly enjoy really long interviews.

The rejection letter was in my mailbox by the time I got home that day, or so it seemed.

The important lesson to take away from this situation, even for a job I really didn't want (their process turned me off), is that you never let your guard down with a recruiter or anyone else in any interview situation. You go for the offer (see Chapter 5) and *then* make the decision about whether to accept the job or not.

It is important to know what doesn't work with recruiters.

- Don't be particularly assertive in follow-ups. If there's a match, and therefore money to be made, the recruiter will find you. When he/she doesn't get back to you after an interview, as many do not, it will almost always mean that either there wasn't a good match or there's been no response from the employer. Persistent following up is not only a waste of time but also may alienate the recruiter. This is not something you want to do, especially if there is the possibility of other options in the future.

- Don't ask for resume or career advice. The only kind of useful resume advice a recruiter will give is to help you accentuate something for a specific employer. Don't let a staffing professional do the rewriting, as you may end up being misrepresented. In terms of career advice, recruiters don't want to feel that you don't know what you want. They want that linear career candidate, not someone who's questioning his or her career goals.

- Don't ask for general coaching, except for specifics about a particular position. The more information you get, the better, although a recruiter may not even know the organizational client well enough to give you solid information, always a clue about your chances on the interview. A weak client relationship means you're not going to be sold well to the client or that you're sent on an interview that isn't a good match.

A frequent major problem with recruiters is their basic mistrust of anyone who's unemployed or trying to change jobs. They prefer candidates they've found by themselves —candidates who are currently employed and happy in their positions. There is sometimes a basic mistrust about why you're on the market, with the assumption there may have been a serious problem on a previous job that would disqualify you. It's their job to try to find this out because he or she certainly doesn't want to sell "damaged goods." You may find yourself on the defensive here, for no reason other than the recruiter is concerned about sending a candidate with a problematic job history. No matter what the reason you're on the market, even if you're still employed, you must have an excellent explanation for this tough audience, a far tougher one than you're likely to encounter in an actual job interview. Your "reason for leaving" statement, as discussed in Chapter 5, has to be airtight. It should be simple, short, and clear. Too much talking about this topic usually implies defensiveness.

I don't want to overemphasize negatives in a particular profession because there are many recruiters who are professional and good at what they do. They best understand that a good placement/good relationship with a candidate is a possible source of future business. The less professional ones see each transaction as a stand-alone deal, not thinking about the long-term business ramifications. Sometimes, a recruiter will make the candidate feel even more like a commodity than is usual in the search process. This latter group may resort to very strong persuasion to close the deal. Sometimes, this kind of recruiter won't even know the particulars of a job, or much about the organizational culture, and will state generalities that may just be designed to persuade the candidate to accept the offer. I strongly urge any candidate to research a company via their own contacts or perhaps through LinkedIn and get information from current employees. I have heard too many stories about prospective employees being misinformed about the actual terms of an offer, as well as imprecise details about the organization.

I think the best way to utilize recruiters as part of an overall search strategy is to treat this group as yet another part of the network. It's a better idea to be referred directly rather than randomly seeking them out. If the source is a client of the recruiter, then you're apt to get more consideration.

Recruiter cover emails are the easiest of all communications in search. This is because most of the recruiters I've known zoom right in on the resume. So the approach/cover email can be very brief, perhaps highlighting three bulleted skills and experiences that will pique the interest of the recruiter. A long, well-crafted cover, I think, is a waste of time. Save those for approaches to your network.

I realize much of what I've written about these two areas of search technique has been negative. In the case of ads, I think the numbers aren't great, and the process primarily random. With recruiters, it's not only a matter of poor odds but also that in many instances, the primary interest of the recruiter is not whether you are the best fit for a new position. Sometimes, they will push so hard to close the deal that the advice will not be helpful or in the client's best interest.

Still, I would like to reiterate that since these techniques do penetrate roughly 12–13% of the total job market, you cannot ignore them.

Chapter 8

Dealing with Unexpected Job Loss

It's reasonable to conclude, based on the statistics showing most people have 12 jobs and three different careers during a work life, that somewhere in there you might lose a job unexpectedly. Maybe it'll be a layoff due to economic difficulties in the organization, personal animosity between boss and employee, or another ridiculously arbitrary reason. But it's going to happen. The studies I've seen indicate it probably will happen around three times in a career. That can include entrepreneurial or consulting ventures as well, where the business may not have worked out. I like to tell clients that if they've gone through it three times already, then they don't have to worry anymore—their quota has been filled —but of course it doesn't quite work like that.

Whatever the circumstance, it is almost always awful to lose a job. It can be devastating and shake your self-esteem to the core. Even when it's a relief after a protracted period of stress, losing a job still represents a loss of structure, loss of economic stability, sometimes loss of status, and maybe loss of your social network, too. Many feel the best way to deal with it is to get the hell out of there as fast as possible and then get going finding a job immediately. This is not necessarily true. Often employers hope you will sign some documents (what's in those documents?), take whatever is offered (if anything is offered), and leave.

Believe it or not, there's some negotiating to be done.

But before this negotiating, the most important thing is, *Don't panic.* Panic is a normal reaction but not one that will work well for you. A common reaction is to automatically think that it's going to be exceedingly difficult to find another job or that whatever economic environment exists at the moment is inopportune for a particular profession. Another typical reaction is to automatically call everyone to let them know what happened, to vent, and to ask for leads and connections. Or to quickly send out hundreds of untargeted resumes. All of this is counterproductive. You should prepare, strategize, and send out a positive message, one that doesn't trash your former employer or convey your desperation and anxiety. You need time to absorb the events, prepare for a job search, and put the best possible marketing spin on your situation. Immediate reaction almost never works well. Call a significant other or a friend for support, and limit it right there. You are now already in networking/branding mode, and you don't want people to feel sorry for you or worse, think you did something terrible. Even if you did have a serious problem at work, do you want that perception out there in your professional or social sphere?

The emotional roller coaster will start. It will take you through something like the stages of grief. Denial, anger, anxiety, apathy, all of it. You should give yourself a few days of doing nothing about getting a search underway except to process what's happened, and maybe even enjoy being out of what may have been a toxic environment. A few days, at most. Many people I've known have instantly started to plan that three-month vacation or the trip around the world, saying, "What the hell, might as well do it now." Sometimes this is a great idea during a career, but it should occur at a time that's been carefully planned, not as the result of something unexpected and certainly not the result of wanting to escape a period of uncertainty.

It's also a good time to rethink the old myth that it's harder to look for a job when you're unemployed. This is simply not true for most people. In fact, it's probably much harder to look for a job when you're employed. After all, how many dentist appointments or family medical emergencies can one person have? When will you have the time to do it right? Effective job search is time-consuming (I think it should take 40–50 hours a week, a full-time job in itself), and unemployed people have a major advantage in this regard. Yes, there are some employers who are suspicious of people who are unemployed, and there is much bad, misleading journalism on this topic. Employers, like everyone else, have wide ranges of behaviors. Even if you have a protracted period of unemployment, there are many excellent ways of explaining it. For example, "I've decided to make this exploration a painstaking, intelligent one where I seek the best fit possible, and if it takes time, so be it." Or if there was just one day of consulting during the unemployment period, that can appear on a resume with the explanation that a consulting assignment came up and was such a good offer you couldn't turn it down. Then, you get to talk about the incredible work you did in that one day, one week, or longer.

Thinking that unemployed people are somehow less qualified is just another one of those rigid, silly thought processes of employers who may have been lucky enough to avoid a termination in their own careers. Or these employers are just rigid, think all careers are linear, and have never given much thought to the fact that most people do not have linear careers. Do you want to work for these people? Do they understand what's really happened in the work world?

What has become of the linear career? I ask groups of students and clients what is the most important quality they seek in a job, and a very common response is "security." That need for security often originates from deep familial roots in the Great Depression, or perhaps it's connected to what many immigrants or international students have experienced in their own countries, or it may come from a personal style where predictability and stability are critical. The Depression created a mindset of working as necessity —you worked or you didn't eat. No safety nets in 1930. This didn't exactly encourage job or career movement. You held on, no matter what. I remember asking my father, who was a product of the Depression, if he liked his work. He looked at me as if I were crazy. "What do you mean 'like'? You live in a nice house, you're going to an expensive private university, so how does 'like' factor into anything?" Liking his work was certainly not a factor in his thinking. He saw work as responsibility, a measure of self-worth and success, but not as something that was supposed to be exciting or challenging.

This attitude, combined with the prosperity of the post-World War II years, created what was supposed to be an ideal work model described in the book, *The Organization Man*—a model that normed the organization as the expected setting for work but implied that men were the only significant players in it. Have you seen the first seasons of *Mad Men*? Seen many women in '50s' movies describing happy professional lives at work? In that world, typified by "Big Blue" IBM, you (a man, of course) subjugated yourself to an organization, got promotions and raises as reward, and then received great benefits for life and maybe a gold watch so that you could enjoy the Golden Years (another interesting '50s'concept). And what you gained was security. Security from the poverty of the Depression. Remember, at that point, only 20 years had passed.

Something changed. It's important to understand why many of us still carry some of the linear notion of careers around with us even now. What changed for many was the attitude toward work, not to mention subsequent economic dislocations. The culture changes in the 1960s and 1970s, probably resulting from a generally more prosperous nation, encouraged questioning about quality of life issues such as "doing your own thing" or the "Me Generation."

Since the 1980s, a changing business climate made the following concepts well known to the general population: leveraged buyouts, mergers, acquisitions, layoffs, entire middle management wipeouts, the breakup of Ma Bell (at least for a little while), and IBM's decimation and reinvention. Later, increasing globalization resulted in the off-shoring of manufacturing and technical jobs. Add to that the hyperinflation and interest rates of 1982, the technology crash of 2000, and the economic meltdown of 2008 and you have a very different business environment than the one my father knew.

The Organization Man has been replaced by the Person with Portfolio. What's evolved is a work concept of incessant change and shifting. People who prefer the idea of lifetime security are probably not going to find it anymore. The organization-for-life paradigm is gone. Over the past several years, this change of work culture has even been evidenced by the large numbers of attorneys and doctors changing professions mid-career. This culture change has affected a large proportion of the working population.

Now that most careers are no longer linear, it's important to recognize that stability, or a sense of security, has to come from within. It has to come from knowing your skills and interests, where you want to be, and how you can best fit a career to your life, with the need for flexibility throughout.

Understanding this new work culture should help you avoid a sense of stigma at being unemployed. "My brother, the accountant, says that no one will look at me if I'm unemployed." Well, your brother just doesn't get it. "My family thinks I'm a loser because I lost my job, even though it was because the company closed." So your family is stuck in Depression/1950s' thinking. They need to get over it, and you need to explain that to them because you need their emotional support. "My husband is frantic that we'll never be able to make the mortgage payment and that I'll never find anything." He needs to be a support, not an additional source of stress. But, most of all, you need to understand that being unemployed is now an expected aspect of a career and has been a part of the regular employment scenario for some time.

Now, on to negotiating your severance. Don't assume that the package offered (if offered) is "take it or leave it." Many of these situations may be negotiable. Though that's toughest when an organization is in financial stress and there have been large numbers of layoffs. Sometimes, employees are asked to leave and pack their belongings in two hours or less, and in some instances, with a security escort. In financially strapped organizations, negotiations are usually about the edges of the package but not the main parts. The most important consideration, no matter what the package or circumstance, is not to sign anything until you review the contents. This is similar to a salary negotiation (at the other end of the employment process), where you ask for time to consider what's being offered and want to take this time to think of any other questions you may have about the conditions of the termination. You're not going to be at your sharpest in such an emotional situation, no matter how resilient you think you are. You need time to strategize. In some organizations, there may be no bending, but you still want clarification on unanswered questions. Remember, what they usually want is for you to sign, leave, and not talk with anyone and potentially disrupt morale. Many organizations do not do this well or tactfully, as evidenced by those two-hour escorted departures, and you need to recognize that it's probably not a personal affront. It's usually about the awkwardness of the person or people facilitating the separation or an organization that does not know how to do it with sensitivity or planning.

The standards for packages vary enormously according to the fiscal health of the organization, the circumstances surrounding the termination, the industry, and the size of the organization. A typical severance package for a middle of the organization employee is two weeks per year of service. For healthier companies, and more senior employees, three weeks per year. For senior people, a month per year, and for those around C-level, the amount has usually been determined by employment contract.

However, as I already mentioned, there are wide variations. For example, the field of advertising does not usually offer as much as indicated above. Large Wall Street law firms, to cite another example that varies from the norm, will frequently offer associates three months of salary continuation, as long as those associates continue to appear in the office and are available to answer questions about their work. Some corporate senior executives are actually paid to stay out of the market (not go to competitors) for a predetermined amount of time. This is called "garden leave." The key to determining what's fair and normal for the industry or organization is to find out from others who have left the company what the precedent has been (whenever possible). Policy precedent is a strong negotiating tool, even better when it's written in an employee manual.

One of the trickier areas of negotiating a severance package is the issue of bonus, if that is a regular component of compensation. If it is, many companies will prorate. Unfortunately, I have seen more than one example where an investment banker has been downsized in November, had many significant deals in the pipeline which he had worked on for many months, and received no bonus. Sometimes, there's a need for an intervention from an employment attorney in these cases or in cases where there's an indication of harassment or discrimination.

Maybe one consultation with an attorney will help with the severance negotiations, so that the attorney can advise you on how to approach the situation or what kind of official letter to write. Usually the attorney will not get directly involved at this juncture because you want to keep the transaction as collegial as possible. If you feel the organization has been unfair, has violated its own protocols or policies, or has behaved in an unlawful way, then maybe more direct involvement with the attorney is required. One important note: it's been my experience that usually the best attorneys to hire are those who only deal with plaintiff-side employment law. You don't want to risk obtaining the services of someone who works on both sides or whose primary clients are corporate. An attorney who specializes in the plaintiff side will be more attuned to your needs. This is definitely not territory for your uncle who practices general law.

Even at this point, with an attorney either advising you on how to communicate with the company or getting more directly involved, it's not necessarily time for a lawsuit. A suit is tough, expensive (as are the previous steps), and can last a long time. My major objection to litigation is that it takes away energies required for job search. But sometimes, it is necessary. Often, though, just the pushback will result in a better package.

Other issues to consider before signing off on any agreement include the following:

- If outplacement services are offered, try to obtain those services from an independent contractor/ provider, who will be able to give you more individual attention than most outplacement firms. The large firms offer a commoditized service—lots of group classes and very little individual attention in general. Individual practitioners are usually less expensive (no major real estate and staff to pay for) and therefore a good way to get the organization to agree to funding someone privately.

- Clarify details about your COBRA coverage or any other benefits continuation. Make sure you understand exactly what services are provided and what the cost is to you. If you are married and your spouse has health coverage, you should compare out-of-pocket costs and coverage levels to determine which option is best for you.

- By law, U.S. companies are only permitted to provide dates of employment in response to external inquiries. You may want to reconfirm this with human resources or personnel, (or talent management, my least favorite euphemism of many), which will remind them that you are aware of the requirement.

- You may also consider writing a departure statement for internal distribution. Something brief that thanks colleagues for their collaboration is appropriate. Remember to keep it positive. Don't use the cliché,

"Have decided to move on to new opportunity." That's a transparent code for "I was terminated."

- Try to make sure your office phone is either cut off or not answered. If possible, have this line forwarded to your cell phone if you feel the need to manage communication with any external constituents about your departure.

- Always backup your personal computer materials regularly at any job. You never know when a company might be bought or closed for some type of malfeasance, or you're going to unexpectedly lose your job. Many times in these instances, you will not get access to your computer and will have difficulty gaining back the private data—if at all.

- Apply for unemployment benefits because you've paid for them. There is no shame in collecting unemployment. You will be leaving money on the table if you don't use this benefit. Most unemployment processes are now automated, so it's common to have to appear at an unemployment office maybe once or twice at most.

You will need to develop the rationale I mentioned in Chapter 5. Regardless of what new opportunities you target, at some point you will be asked by a potential employer or contact why you left your previous job. Whereas layoffs/terminations are a common fact of life, it is extremely important to think carefully about how you want to frame a response to this inquiry. No matter what the cause, the reason has to reflect positively on you and the former employer. Focus on why you are a great fit for the opportunity at hand, or emphasize what you know and what your experience has been. Hiring managers and networking contacts want to hear about what you can offer, so emphasize your value proposition and the skills that enable you to meet the needs of the marketplace.

If you plan to use references from your former company, you need to be comfortable with what each person will say about you. Whenever you give a name to a potential employer, you should contact anyone providing a reference to clarify how you want to position yourself. Also, don't abuse the privilege by giving the same reference dozens of times. You want to keep these relationships intact, so use them judiciously. Do not supply references on an initial application or screening interview. It's too early and you risk abusing the references since you don't even know if the situation is serious yet. State that you'll be happy to supply the references at a more advanced stage in the conversation but that these people are very important to you and you don't want to take advantage. This usually is sufficient. Make sure you're comfortable with your references. Any hesitation on the other end of a request may lead to one of those "damning by faint praise" references.

You will need to manage your expectations reasonably. The recent economic climate means that your search may take longer than you anticipated, especially if you are looking to transition at an experienced/lateral level, where many organizations have slowed the hiring process. If you aspire to make a significant career change, either by switching industries or functional areas or both, the process may be more difficult, as hiring managers will undoubtedly be more risk averse in their assessment of candidates. Consequently, think carefully about your job targets and consider "bridge" opportunities in addition to more secure backup jobs. (More about this in Chapter 9.) If you need to earn income immediately, this is not the time to focus on a major career change. Instead, find work in an area that immediately taps your skills and experience and then begin the process of exploring longer-term goals once your personal financial bases are covered.

Whatever you do, try to remain careful, strategic, and professional during this stressful time. How you handle an unexpected job loss can determine the success of your next move.

Chapter 9

Bridge Jobs

Let's assume that you've just finished a degree or certification because you were (a) interested in the subject and (b) confident the credential would prepare you well for the job market. You had done significant research prior to application and enrollment to determine what the job market would look like after completion. With your strategy in place, you had pretty good job search skills and were ready to go, convinced you had made an excellent decision in choosing the course of study and career direction based on a careful self-assessment. But . . . maybe you weren't quite as thorough as you had thought, given the numerous unpredictable variables involved.

You find out, much to your surprise, that it's more difficult to get the job than you expected, despite the excellent education, the series of summer internships, and the previous job experience. It's pointed out to you over and over that you're "missing" something; there's some gap in your skills and/or experience. This is immensely discouraging after all the hard work, preparation, and, more than likely, huge student loan debt. You're sure it's not your search strategy because you've heard from several of the people you've contacted—and trusted—that there really is a deficit in your training and background. What to do? There has to be a way to fill in that gap.

Before deciding on a course of action, it's important to get past the frustration of completing the training, spending the money, and working hard to get to this point in a search, only to find out there is yet another step to take. This is a normal part of career development. Frustrating? Yes. Predictable? Yes. Possible to avoid every time? No.

The first step in addressing the gap is to figure out what's missing. Which skill? What kind of experience? It's important to stick to the notion of critical mass addressed in Chapter 3 on networking, which is that you never believe anything unless you've heard it repeated from several trusted sources. Usually, a pattern will emerge, if not total unanimity. For example, four out of six contacts will suggest one idea; a fifth will suggest another that is completely different; and a sixth will say there is no market for you at all and no jobs out there. (Remember the "lazy and stupid" networking contact discussed earlier? That's this sixth person.) With the four out of six ideas about your deficits, you have critical mass.

Now you have something to go on. An important skill or experience is missing from your portfolio. Before rushing to get that skill, first test out other information sources to be certain this is something you must attain. This means going back to the network once again to try to confirm the new assessment. It's important to attain that critical mass of opinion in order to make an intelligent decision.

The solution requires some creative thinking.

After you've pinpointed the gap, you'll need to figure out methods for gaining the missing experience and/or skill. One technique is to ask a contact, former classmate, or friend in the industry you're targeting if this person could use any assistance on a project. Think like a consultant in all of your conversations with people in your target area. Find out what they need by listening attentively when they're discussing their work, and then come up with suggestions about how you might be able to help. This is pro bono, but once you've completed this project, you could list it on your resume as a consulting assignment, detailing the skills that were previously missing. Before you begin, make sure the person you're collaborating with approves of your listing the assignment as consulting.

Another way to gain the missing experience is to get either a paid or unpaid internship, which you would find via your network. It's important to negotiate a few issues at the beginning of such an arrangement, especially if it's unpaid. Otherwise, it may turn out to be a waste of time. For example, be sure to ask if it's okay to list the internship as a consultancy, which sounds better than internship. Internship often connotes a more junior position than what you're trying to accomplish—especially if you're mid-career.

Ask if you could be introduced to the employer's contacts and receive an excellent reference upon completion of the internship, assuming, of course, that your work has been superior. This is a great way to let the employer know you intend not only to do a terrific job but also that you want to make sure others will find out about it.

Sometimes internships get tricky, involving a kind of bait and switch. You're told you're going to have certain responsibilities, and you end up at Kinko's several hours each day. Go over the responsibilities before you start, giving a clear message that you're there for a specific reason.

Additionally, you should ask at the beginning whether there might be an opportunity for full-time employment at the conclusion of the internship. While this is unlikely, there's certainly no harm in asking. As I ask many clients in job search, "What do you have to lose?" Sometimes, internships may be a "try and buy" situation with both sides trying each other out, and the position could turn into a real job.

A successful bridge job will fill in the gap, give credibility, and add the needed credential. But it could accomplish more. Every setting is an opportunity for building networks. Interning or project work in an organization will put you into a setting where you can meet people, many of whom might be working in precisely the area you are targeting. A whole new network. Maybe even possibilities for employment.

A few years ago, I was advising a student at Columbia Business School. She was an administrator at the Medical

Center at the university—a pretty senior role with a great deal of responsibility. Bored with her job, she had come to Columbia to figure out how she might leverage her skills and background into a more senior and challenging role.

Like many students in graduate school, she changed her mind halfway through the program, realizing that not only was she most talented in the financial areas of her current job but also that she liked finance more than any other course she had taken. Therefore, she planned to take more finance courses, (as many as possible), before she graduated. Her grades were excellent, and she was gaining recognition for her drive and overall intelligence. She gradually realized, after due diligence on her options, that she wanted to go into investment banking.

Yes, there was a significant gap in her impressive experience at the hospital—not enough finance experience she could leverage into banking. She had good experience but not the right kind. From her extensive networking she knew she would need to gain relevant experience to back up her candidacy for the type of job she wanted.

She eventually concluded that she needed an internship at a bank. I advised her that this would not only be difficult (she had missed the on-campus recruiting cycle) but also presented the logistical problem—how could she simultaneously keep her job and do the internship? Her answer? She would quit her job and take the leap.

I forgot to mention that she was a single parent, just in case anyone reading this is thinking it was going to be easy. But she was determined to make it work.

She had saved a substantial amount of money, her tuition was paid for, and she was ready to try. Utilizing her already impressive network, she managed to land an internship at one of the major banks. This took months and involved several iterations of how she would leverage her previous experience and make it relevant to organizations that maintained highly competitive requirements for hiring. And she didn't have the benefit of the campus recruiting system, itself a highly difficult process.

As if all this wasn't impressive enough, she continued her graduate program while working in the internship. Within two months, they offered her a full-time job. An amazing story and a great demonstration of creative thinking and tenacity.

The bridge jobs I've described demonstrate how to fill in credential gaps. But there is a different kind of bridging that will help you achieve similar goals.

Several years ago, I had a client in his mid-30s who had a successful career working in technology for a well-known electronics corporation. He wanted to get into media, completely motivated by a need to make more money. His primary goal was to "be where the money is," as he articulated it. He also liked the idea of the entertainment industry. He had done limited research into what it would take for him to reach his goal; he only knew he wanted to make the switch.

I recognized it would be a tough transition. His English wasn't very good, and his thinking was a little rigid. He thought getting an MBA would be the solution and the degree alone would lead to employment in his target area. In other cultures, like his for example, that is indeed the case. I explained to him it didn't usually work that way in the United States but there might be a better way. I also had to explain that an on-campus recruiting program would not look at him as a prime candidate because of his age (they primarily target students in their mid- to late-20s for a variety of reasons) and experience. Also, media companies didn't frequently recruit on campus. What I didn't want to tell him yet was that he would need to be more flexible in learning about requirements and necessary skills for becoming a media professional or that his potential market might be limited. He already found the whole proposition quite daunting, and sometimes too much information and advice can be hard to hear. He needed to come to the correct conclusions on his own.

He came back to my office after completing his MBA, shaken and demoralized. He had not found any traction in his search and blamed his business school for "not finding me a job." I pointed out to him that it wasn't the school's role to find him a job but rather to provide the resources and training that would enable him to succeed.

This was the right time to also point out the kind of bridge jobs that would make it possible to get where he wanted. I suggested he find a job in one of the media companies in his area of technology. I explained that one of the best ways to bridge is to leverage previous experience, then build networks internally and use the platform to try to move inside the organization. This was especially feasible for technology professionals, since they worked with "users" (professionals on the business side who were their clients). I had seen many technology professionals make these transitions. The key was the ability to develop relationships, not something that came easily for this client.

We talked at length and he finally came around after significant resistance to the idea of continuing to work in his old field. Basic networking was not only uncomfortable for his personal style but also was culturally counterintuitive. Once inside the media company, it took him quite some time to develop a network, but ultimately, he moved into a position that he targeted. This was a significant success for him on many levels, being able to move past cultural, personal, and career barriers.

I can imagine some readers thinking, "Easy for him to say, 'Get a bridge job.' What about making money to pay back those loans? I also have to live. How can I bridge *and* make money? I definitely cannot afford to do an unpaid internship or pro bono project." The answer is either to bridge by utilizing a former skill in a setting where you can move internally, or, if there's a financial pressure, to take a job just to make money. This is the third type of bridge.

The best kind of expedient bridging, in which you make money immediately, is to find something—anything

—in an organization that is in some way connected to your target. If you're a human resources professional from a corporation and want to eventually move into an environmental nonprofit as a program manager, and you want no part of human resources in your long-term planning, then perhaps a human resources position in either an environmental non-profit or *any* non-profit will be your bridge. In this way, you obtain the credential of working in your target area or something close to it. What you want is credibility in the nonprofit arena, which will be the bridge to your eventual target. The point is that you will try to get any kind of job that's reasonably acceptable to you and is in something close to your target.

As if all this bridging isn't frustrating enough— prolonging the attainment of your goal—there's one more important consideration. As in any new job, you give yourself a honeymoon period. No ambitious networking or job search at the beginning; just get settled in and established in the new position. Give yourself a break from the grind of the search, too, unless something else is already in process.

For three months. That's when the serious discipline must kick in and it's time to build networks inside the organization. Yes, it's back to the search. Or, if the organization is not within your target area, you start to build those relationships outside the organization. But this time, you are operating from a platform within the target industry (in this case, nonprofit).

You'll have something better to leverage than you had before. A better bridge.

I don't mean to suggest that there's always a solution; sometimes markets dictate that certain fields at a given time do not have many openings. From 2009 to now (2013), real estate development anywhere in the United States has been extremely difficult to penetrate, even for those with extensive experience. But, in a good search, that real estate professional will have a B or C fallback plan. My main focus on bridge jobs is to emphasize that there usually is a way to get to the goal, even if there seems to be major obstacles.

Chapter 10

Creating Your Own Job Search Style: A Success Story

Let's get this out of the way up front. Job search is dreadful. I have never believed career transition is a self-discovery mission or some kind of spiritual journey. Many popular books and articles liken this process to some kind of religious experience. It most certainly is not. The process is usually awful. In fact, it's probably one of the few situations in life worse than dating. Where else can you encounter so much arbitrary personal rejection? Yes, you might learn things about yourself and find out about careers and jobs you might not have known about otherwise. But it's also isolating and grindingly hard work, enough to test anyone's fortitude. The only truly good part is when it's over.

I like to use one client's story as an example of how you can make your job search work for you (instead of the other way around) and alleviate *some* of the unpleasantness that can accompany this process.

The Beginning

Ann was a senior vice president at one of the major New York City megabanks (one that was too big to fail). She had been with the organization for twelve years and was completely unprepared for the layoff that eliminated her job. Her field was always among the first to be cut in downturns, thereby making this a tough transition in the midst of difficult economic times. To complicate matters further, she was 58 years old and single with a small personal network, much of it internal to the organization she was leaving.

The situation did not look promising. When she first came into my office, my immediate thoughts centered on alternative career options that would probably pay less and be less challenging. But, I didn't yet know about her strength and determination in pursuing her goals. Forgive the spoiler, but this is a success story. Her success was largely based on the use of social media, especially LinkedIn. I had thought of LinkedIn as one of a wide variety of tools job seekers could utilize; with Ann, it was the method that made the difference.

Like many who have lost their jobs in large organizations, Ann felt she had plenty of time and a decent severance package as buffer to look within the organization. She was encouraged by colleagues, human resources, and friends within the organization, which is typical in these situations. But I was skeptical about her chances, having heard many stories on this subject from other clients. And the people who encouraged her certainly did not want any of the laid-off employees to feel that they didn't have a chance.

I frequently tell clients to focus on both the internal and external markets, knowing that the internal searches during a time of mass layoffs are going to be difficult. Often, internal recruiting perceives the employee as "damaged goods," whether or not that has any validity, which helps to explain most companies' preference for outside hires over internal. The new seems somehow preferable, or maybe more exciting, than the old. For some reason, there is a mystique that the outside candidate will be superior to the talent they could develop internally. The significant culture knowledge of the internal candidate may be overlooked.

It's emotionally wrenching to separate from an organization in the first place but even more difficult when you've been there for 12 years. Ann stuck too long with her internal search. (One of the most important things I've learned is that clients are ready precisely when they are ready, despite any insistent pushing on my part, or anyone else's.) When she finally reached a dead end, she was ready to start her external search.

Getting Started

Ann began by researching all the financial services and related organizations that would have the kind of department she wished to join. She wanted to stay in her field, despite knowing it would be tough to find something appropriate. She used Hoovers and several other databases to begin compiling lists of companies. She updated her profile on LinkedIn, learning how to do that from various sites online. She contacted executive recruiters, not a very high-odds proposition in a bad market but sometimes useful. She joined professional associations to help build her small network beyond her former organization. Two of these were particularly useful and continued to be throughout the search. Professional organizations with regular events and committees one can join are a quick way to build networks. They frequently provide a great jump start for someone like Ann, who might not have an extensive personal network.

She developed approach emails and worked hard on her self-marketing pitch. Developing the pitch, along with editing her resume and emails, helped her realize she had a great deal to sell. Job loss can have a terrible effect on self-confidence so it's critical to develop self-marketing materials at the outset. A well-crafted email approach, a well-targeted pitch, and an easy-to-read resume does wonders for confidence. After they have reviewed and practiced self-marketing techniques, I love to ask clients and students, "So do you actually *believe* this now?" Of course, they do; it's a matter of reconnecting with what they've accomplished in their careers.

As Ann said repeatedly, she was "relentless," never reaching out just once to someone she wanted to meet but at least three times. One technique she created was to resend an original email "with a twist," something she called her "apology email," which she estimates received a positive response at least 95% of the time. ("I do apologize for yet another email. However, I am doing some market research for my job search and welcome the opportunity to meet with you.") I don't know why this worked so well, but I cannot argue with its consistent success. This is a great example of that "out of the box" thinking that is a major asset in many searches.

Highly organized, she used spreadsheets to track her job search activities. As I've mentioned before, being organized helps a great deal by letting you feel more in control over a situation where it's tough to feel much control. And it keeps you from losing track of important follow-ups. As Ann has said about her search many times, "Networking became a way of life." At one point, Ann had more than 500 contacts, which ended up in about 200 job leads overall.

Social Media

Ann proved that LinkedIn could be a powerful job search tool. She started with about 20 connections which quickly grew to 150. But the number of contacts doesn't mean that much. Many think that the "500+" imprimatur on LinkedIn actually means something significant; it doesn't. She connected with those people she felt could help her directly and joined several groups—not necessarily to discuss issues but to find potential leads.

Often people think the purpose of LinkedIn is to make direct contacts with that friend of a friend of a friend to get introductions. This technique does work for many people but it involves getting introductions from that "level 2" person to the "level 1" and takes time and patience. Ann learned how to find email addresses and phone numbers for those who were not listed on LinkedIn. ("Switchboard research" involves calling the general company phone number and figuring out emails from a prototype on a company website.)

Through sheer determination and the realization that this is largely a numbers game, she found some contacts who took an interest in helping. Sometimes these contacts had been on job search themselves recently; these were often people who may have had excellent ideas and further connections that were viable and current.

Ann spent several hours a day "trolling" through LinkedIn connections. She would sometimes see an email address of a major department head through other connections. She was able to get an excellent informational interview and contacts that eventually led to her two job offers—both of them from people she had not known before. She did not use introductions in most of her LinkedIn reaching out. Her approaches on LinkedIn were almost all direct.

I think it's important to mention here that Ann did not sit in her apartment researching LinkedIn and her other resources 16 hours a day. She was determined to feel good, look good, and lower the stress level by going to her gym almost daily, seeing friends, etc. Maintaining a good work/ life balance during search is critical. Too often I've seen people not pay enough attention to maintaining this balance; the ensuing stress levels often result in less productivity.

The Meetings

Ann said she prepared for her meetings "as if I were studying for a course." Her research was extensive. Sometimes she had a better knowledge of a company than the people who worked there. Part of her preparation for an informational meeting was to check out the company website for job openings, and if she saw one that was relevant, she geared her pitch to that job. She also checked out the investor relations presentations on the websites, which gave her further valuable information. Most important of all, Ann, who was an excellent active listener, used what she heard in order to craft appropriate questions and follow-ups that demonstrated how she could add value to a company or a referral. Ann also took detailed notes and kept records of all her search activities.

Ann even handled the roller coaster of search well, usually one of the toughest parts because you're functioning in isolation and getting little in the way of feedback. It's difficult to keep the energy going. Frequently people drop out during the summer or the holidays in December—a critical mistake because you can lose momentum as well as opportunities for building networks. Ann made the best of what normally is one of the hardest times of the year for job seekers—the second half of December. She thought of a way to get past that with her "Happy Holiday" email campaign. She saw it as a great chance to put herself in front of her contacts, and she personalized every message. Her notes led to a few interviews and meetings, one of which turned into an offer.

Ann also had her share of disappointments, particularly with one company where she had actually assisted the human resources director in writing the job description. She was following through on her *quid pro quo* promise, "If I ever can be of help to you, as you were with me, please do not hesitate to call." She had developed what appeared to be a strong relationship with the director, and she stayed in constant contact with him throughout eight rounds of interviews. The company never got back to her, despite her several attempts at following up, and apparently never filled the position. That one was tough to get past and extremely discouraging. Ann had done everything right; one of the awful lessons of search is that doing it right doesn't necessarily mean every situation will work out.

In situations like this one, where the company handles the recruiting process in a less than professional manner, it's usually better for the job to fall away than to have received the offer.

The Landing

Through a series of referrals, Ann met with a major consulting company. The managing director thought she should broaden her pitch and that she wouldn't be a good fit in his area. He did, however, question his own initial impression and referred her to several people on his staff, intrigued by what she might bring to the company. At the same time, she found another consulting company opening, where again it was suggested that she broaden her presentation.

After many interviews, Ann received an offer from the first consulting company, and she turned it down. This surprised me after her ten-month search. But she was not happy about the amount of travel involved. While this took an enormous amount of courage, she felt she had figured out exactly what the right setting would be and didn't want to settle for a position she knew wouldn't be the right one.

The second consulting company, where she is now completing her sixth month, offered her a position as well. The interviewing process was long and arduous, seven different interviews and a shift from one area to another in the company. The job paid her more than she made at the bank, and although it was initially overwhelming, she was thrilled to be with an excellent organization in an interesting and diverse culture.

Here's my favorite part of the story. As a result of her prodigious efforts, she had at least two or three potential job situations in the works at the time she accepted the consulting firm offer. She feels, with great confidence, that even if this new job doesn't work out, she would be able to land another quickly. I don't doubt it.

Of course, someone reading this chapter might think there was no way he or she could do what Ann did. I would never suggest that a job seeker has to take the same route. She was guided by her own style and inclinations and utilized tools that suited her.

Over the years, I have frequently been asked about the "right" way to do a search. Many people are seeking the perfect formula, when there isn't one. They want $X+Y = $ New Perfect Job, when in reality this process is much more art than science. Yes, there are certain basics that need to be learned (correspondence, resume, pitch, skillfully utilizing networks, interview technique, negotiations, etc.). But putting it all together requires some creativity, an expression of the individual's unique style. That's exactly what Ann demonstrated.

Even if you could never do what Ann did, here's what I hope you'll take away from her story:

- LinkedIn is a great resource for information, not just connections.

- Follow-up is the key to success in making connections.

- A job search is a sales campaign.

- Know your audience. Adjust your marketing materials and presentation to each one individually.

- Discipline and consistency make all the difference.

Note: For those who want to get up to speed quickly on using social media for career transition, I highly recommend Rob Hellmann's e-book, *Your Social Media Job Search* (robhellmann.com).

In Search of the Forever-Fun Job

Chapter 11

Do You Ever Get to Burn Bridges?
Developing Strategies for Coping with the
Emotional Roller Coaster

During one of my difficult career transitions, I was amazed, again and again, by some of the strange or bad behavior I encountered. Even after all these years, I continue to be surprised by what we at Columbia Business School call poor "social intelligence."

One of my coping mechanisms during that difficult search was to plan to burn bridges by the dozen the minute I turned 60. I would tell all the people who had shown a lack of courtesy or seriously bad behavior, exactly what I thought. I figured that at 60, it simply wouldn't matter anymore—burning a bridge or two wouldn't affect my career and by that age, I would have earned the right to do it. This sounded great. This notion led me to accumulate, through experiences with clients and students, some other coping mechanisms as well.

As I hope I have made clear in this book, there is nothing particularly illuminating, spiritual, or gratifying about career transitions—except for (usually) the end product. Maybe you meet some interesting people along the way and gain interesting insights about yourself but that's about it. Even then, a great outcome can feel anti-climactic. A relief, maybe, but not necessarily the anticipated thrill. Many years ago, I taught a course at New York University, The Nuts and Bolts of Job Search. I always began the course by saying to the students, "Write this down: 'Job search sucks.' And don't forget it." It was important for me to quickly disabuse clients and students of the idea that this process was some form of life-affirming self-discovery. All the rejection and uncertainty is hard to take, especially when you're already feeling anxious and worried. Knowing that you will experience a great deal of unpleasant and insensitive behavior during a search can help you get through the process without too many low moments.

Everyone needs techniques for dealing with this experience, so I'm offering a few. Some I arrived at on my own; others are borrowed from clients and students.

Build Structures

If you've lost a job, a huge part of your daily structure is gone. Maybe you can enjoy a little time off from all the stress of whatever preceded the unemployment, but you need to create new structures. Building a day around laundry and other errands just won't do past the first week or so. As I have mentioned, physical exercise, built into every day, is critical. And the job search itself, if executed in a disciplined, consistent, systematic manner, should provide an excellent structure for each day. Whenever I meet a new client who doesn't know what to do with all the free time, I know right away that this person doesn't know how to do a search. It should be like a job—all day, every day, with a few rewards and exercise breaks thrown in—and, yes, some time to do errands. One of the most difficult aspects of search for many is that it is inherently isolating. Try to build in some lunches and other occasions with friends on a regular basis.

Think About When You Might Actually Burn Bridges

"Never burn a bridge," is an often repeated business cliché. Roughly translated it means you're supposed to resist the anger and the temptation to say what you really want to say. It means, don't show what you're really thinking. Be a grownup.

Several years ago, as I mentioned, I thought that when I was reasonably secure in my career, I could actually burn a few bridges. Maybe tell some ridiculous corporate human resources professional half my age and absurdly arrogant and/or incompetent what I really thought of his ineptness. There have been many opportunities.

It was, and still is, a great fantasy. Thinking about what I wanted to say always made me feel better.

But now I'm past the point I used to think would have earned me the right to burn bridges. Even though I've faced the temptation many times, I've always resisted the urge to follow through. Let me give you just a few examples of situations where those bridge fires might have been set.

One comes from a friend of mine, let's call her Jane, who worked for one of the most difficult managers I've ever heard about (and I've unfortunately heard many astonishing examples). The manager was consistently abusive, a screamer, wildly irrational, and horribly controlling. She used Jane as a go-between for abusing other members of the organization, putting my friend in an untenable situation. For many reasons, including a very good compensation package and coworkers with whom she formed very strong, positive relationships, Jane stayed on the job for way too many years. The behavior of the manager became progressively worse; it was the type of relationship that goes beyond my expertise to explain.

Jane finally found another job. She had been planning the day of her departure for a long time (another great fantasy), anticipating that she would go to the board of the organization and tell them everything, excoriating the manager personally for all the years of terrible behavior.

She chose not to. I'm not sure why, but it did work out unexpectedly well for her.

They stayed in touch, and the manager was actually able to help Jane in her new job in an area where my friend lacked a degree of expertise. The manager continued to be an excellent resource for Jane. It turned out she was actually much easier to work with when she wasn't my friend's manager.

Let me give you another example of why you want to leave those bridges intact, even after the age of 60.

Last year, I took on a corporate-sponsored outplacement client. She had left the firm in good standing; her separation was the result of the company's poor economic situation. She told me that the executive vice president of human resources had already given his approval for her to use my services instead of the outplacement firm that had been offered. All I needed was an approval in writing from him. Then I would send him a proposal or description of the program if he needed one.

I wrote to him immediately, since my client wanted to get started as soon as possible. She was highly anxious about doing a search because she had been with this company for a very long time and had not refined her search skills while she was there. The last time she had looked for a job, she was at entry level; now she was a senior vice president of a prestigious Wall Street technology company. She knew this search was going to be different from her last one.

The HR executive did not respond to my email. I wrote again because I couldn't start with the client until I had written approval from him, a form of contract. After still not hearing from him, I suggested she call him herself, and if that failed, get her manager (the CEO) to get him to respond.

Still no response.

Three or four weeks after the verbal approval to the client, I received a terse email, "You can go ahead with the program." No salutation, no nothing. Just one sentence and a signature. Again, I wrote back stating the fee and some of the details of the program (in which he showed no interest at any point). I needed written approval not only of the program itself but also of the fee.

He took another week to get back to me. My client, about whom he should have been far more concerned, was extremely upset that her program had been delayed a month. The HR executive had created a bad feeling both with the former senior executive and with me, not good branding for him or his company.

It got worse during the few months of the program. Without getting into more detail, the HR executive not only was uncommunicative but also did not pay the bill. I ended up writing to him about five times to at least get an acknowledgment of the invoice; the actual payment took much longer.

I resolved, once paid, to burn this bridge with a nuclear weapon. I was going to write to the CEO. And if that didn't get a good enough response, maybe a letter to all the members of the company's board.

Somehow, once I was paid, it became less important, and I realized I'd never do business with this guy again anyway, so it didn't seem worth the effort.

A few weeks ago, I received a call from someone else at the same company, same program, same issues with outplacement. Another decent program and because I hadn't burned the bridge to this extremely unprofessional executive, a totally unexpected piece of business. The same HR executive approved the program, but, of course, I haven't heard from him yet. Yes, it will be annoying to deal with him again, but I never would have received the repeat business if I'd responded out of anger in the previous situation. The burned bridge would have caused me to lose potential business, even at this point. Dealing with people like that comes with the territory of doing business.

Each time I've been on the verge of articulating what I really think, I stop myself and realize it just wouldn't accomplish anything, except perhaps compromising my own integrity. Plus, it would harm my professional standards and reputation. So, I've fought the urge and let most of those impulses go. I might not follow-up as much as I used to with a prospective corporate client, when the thought of working with that person is intolerable to me, but this is really more an act of silence than a bridge burning.

Who knows? Perhaps one of these days, I actually will follow through. It's so tempting. In the meantime, planning to burn a bridge is a wonderful way to deal with the frustrations of putting yourself out there.

The Shit List

Okay, I've watched my language for this entire book, but there's just no other way of explaining this list.

I learned this technique from a client and think it's terrific. Very similar to the fantasy of burning bridges but with a little twist.

You're going to meet people on a search who will either think they're superior because they have a job (ridiculous), enjoy passing judgment, or think they have a right to express opinions, no matter how wrong or unnecessary. You'll also meet terrific people, which I need to say here before we get going with the revenge fantasies.

This particular client kept a running list of people he met during a protracted search—people he thought behaved unprofessionally or discourteously. His search was tough and lasted far too long—mainly due to a difficult market in his target area. Then he met a woman who worked in a firm where he had tried for months to gain access. He had heard that the woman would be a great networking resource and would have helpful advice.

He was excited to make this contact and prepared well for the meeting. But almost from the start, he knew something was wrong. The woman was unwelcoming and seemed annoyed that she had to be there. After a few minutes, he actually asked her if she wanted to continue the meeting, since she seemed preoccupied. She replied, "Let's get this over with." Of course there was no way the meeting would be successful; something was clearly off. But my client persisted, asked some questions and did his best to present himself in the most positive way. The woman told him she didn't believe he belonged in the field at all and that people with his background never succeeded in it. She had nothing encouraging to say. (Ironically, he found out later they had almost identical backgrounds. It is also important to add that he later achieved a significant level of success in the field she so conclusively felt he was wrong for.)

He was devastated by the meeting, though it was obvious her response had little or nothing to do with anything he had said or presented. Something was clearly wrong even before they met. She presented her opinions in a cruel and demeaning way. Even if someone in her position believed those things, why would she express them so tactlessly to a total stranger—one who was referred by a friend of hers?

She rose to the top of "the list." He was not a vengeful person but hoped she might find out, someday, that she had been unnecessarily dismissive with a person who had come to her for support and information during a difficult personal time.

Several years later, he was active in his professional association and was responsible for vetting candidates for open board positions every year. His committee submitted her name for approval, and he almost started to laugh. He remembered her name well—top of the list. The revenge factor took over. He told the group he had never vetoed anyone running for the board and this would be the first. And . . . would everyone in the room please do their best to make sure she knew who had cast the veto?

This is one of the few times I've heard when "the list" did result in a measure of concrete satisfaction, a "what goes around, comes around" story. Job seekers need not spend valuable time planning revenge on those who behaved offensively, but I do love the idea of maintaining "the list."

Draft the Response You *Really* Want to Write But Won't

This one, too, is a fantasy, but it's also a satisfying mental exercise.

A young client, recent college graduate, struggled in his first job search, an all-too-common situation these days. He was bright, highly articulate, and for a 22-year-old, reasonably well-credentialed with a terrific, infectious sense of humor.

He was not focused at this point (like many his age) but executed a good search in a couple of areas. He applied for an interesting administrative job at a prestigious New York City law school. He felt he had done well on the interview and was eagerly awaiting a response. As with most interviewing situations, the decision makers rarely contact applicants when they say they will. (This is, I think, an unspoken fact of any career transition. People will never get back to you when they say they will.) I advised him to follow-up, which he did.

He received the response, "Thanks for your message. We are still in the process of interviewing candidates for the position so have not yet made any decision. However, we have several who have significantly more relevant experience than you, so unfortunately, it is unlikely we will make you an offer. If you have any further questions, please do not hesitate to reach out to me."

And here's *my* question: Why in the world would a decision maker send such a condescending note to an applicant, telling him there were better applicants? What does this accomplish? There are so many things wrong with this communication, but I'm wandering off the main topic here. How do you cope with such behavior?

Writing a response to this kind of communication is fun. My client wrote an obscene email (not sent, of course), but it was funny as hell and was a great way to vent.

Sometimes, I think there's a book of letters someone should write—the ones you wish you could have sent. Think of all the possibilities! You could comment on how the parents of the potential employer should have thought twice before this particular conception, or maybe there's something you'd like to say about the person's personal appearance or sartorial decisions. If you're feeling up to a more mature effort, a witty repudiation of all the comments made in the rejection email or critiquing the person's grammar would feel good.

I have an even worse example. Another client, an accomplished and brilliant 35-year-old man was told by an executive at a major New York City investment bank that he was the lead candidate for a position and an offer would be forthcoming. Something about the interview process led me to believe the interviewer was a little off, and the client should think carefully about taking such a position if offered.

Unfortunately, I was right. My client followed up at least three times over the course of a month, since, as I mentioned, he'd been told he was going to get an offer. No response. That would make this story bad enough, but there was an eventual response by email:

> Hi Jim,
> Unfortunately, we already have candidate
> with better match for position.
> Al

No one could make this up. Aside from the poor language skills, this prospective employer felt the need to tell my client he had found someone "better"! *After* telling him he was going to get an offer. Again, what was the point of a communication like this? My client, an introverted guy who had difficulty marketing himself, was having a prolonged and stressful search. What kind of branding was this for both the manager and for the organization he represented? I did convince my client he was better off not working for this guy. I always think if such behavior in the recruiting process represents the best foot forward, who wants to see the rest of the body?

My client seriously thought about writing to the manager's boss—someone he knew and had been his original referral source (making his story even more outrageous, if possible)—but I told him there was no point. He did draft something, and it was scathing. He felt much better after that. He addressed, point by point, why the decision was wrong, why the company was going to lose out by not hiring him, and, most importantly, why the email he had received was unprofessional and portrayed the sender in a very negative way.

These are just some of the coping techniques you can use to maintain your perspective and equilibrium during a tough time. Try to keep in mind that everyone in transition is going to encounter negative behaviors no matter what. Don't take it personally. You need to stay even, avoid the roller coaster, and, like sales people, move on to your next possible opportunity.

In Search of the Forever-Fun Job

Epilogue:

Just One More Thing

I wanted to take this one last opportunity to remind you that while career transition is difficult, it's also eminently doable. I'm no cheerleader (ask my clients), but I have yet to meet a client or student who didn't succeed as a result of doing the hard work I've talked about in this book. Of course, there are many variables, including personality type, credentials, and market conditions, but I know from experience that if you carefully research your targets and use strong search techniques that include reading the job markets as you proceed, you will make your task easier. And if you learn to manage the emotional roller coaster, the whole process won't be so painful. Will you find a job that's fun forever? Maybe not. But once you add in those final essential ingredients—consistency and discipline—you will have everything you need for success. I wish you the best of luck.

Please visit my website, www.ellischase.com, for more job search resources.

In Search of the Forever-Fun Job

Acknowledgments

Three of the people closest to me have been significantly responsible for my being able to write—and eventually complete—*In Search of the Fun-Forever Job*. Of course, my clients and students have also provided so much of the material.

Michele Orwin, who has been my very close friend for over 50 years (inconceivable), insisted that I had something to say when I didn't really believe it. She cajoled (in her very gentle and careful way), shaped, edited, and managed the project from the beginning. She even helped me to actually like writing. Okay, so it took a few years. She's one of the two genuine, real live writers involved in this. I learned that writers are very patient people and have this ability to look at a paragraph, change a couple of words here and there, and make the thing work.

My wife, Carola, has always been a terrific editor and writer. Brutal, at times, but impressive in her intuitive understanding of economy and structure of language. She's been editing my articles for years and has reviewed every aspect of this work multiple times. I never react well when I see the edits, but . . . she makes my ramblings coherent.

Hannah, my daughter, was the inspiration for this book. It has stuck in my mind that her writing effort when she was around eight, *The Fun-Forever Job*, was eventually—about 20 years later—going to be the lynchpin of a book. Her career evolution has been the color informing much of my thinking about the career "epiphanies" that I love to talk about.

It would be difficult not to include Lorraine Fico-White on this page. Even after all the years of encouragement and professional know-how of Michele Orwin, the inspiration from Hannah Chase, and the word-by-word reshaping by Carola Chase, the end product worked because of Lorraine's remarkable ability to see inside the words and thoughts and make them work by shaping, reshaping, and eventually achieving coherence. Amazing.

About the Author

Ellis Chase, one of Manhattan's top career consultants and executive coaches, brings his 25-plus years of experience and expertise to this reexamination of how to target and find a job that fits.

Known for his irreverent style, Ellis cuts through the clutter and clichés of what passes for conventional wisdom to offer a real-life, direct approach to job hunting and career development—an approach more in line with today's economic realities.

Ellis's varied consulting practice is based in Manhattan, but his workshops and presentations often have taken him around the United States and Europe. His corporate clients have included the following companies: Deloitte Touche, Estee Lauder, Goldman Sachs, The Gartner Group, Purdue Pharma, Swiss Re America, United Nations Development Programmes, Penguin Putnam, Citigroup, WR Wrigley, ING Capital, Group M, Amnesty International, American Civil Liberties Union, Hanger Orthopedics, and Time Warner.

He has been a consultant to Columbia Business School for the past 11-plus years where he develops curricula and delivers workshops for the Business School's Executive MBA Career Management and Alumni Relations Career Services; he coaches in the Program for Social Intelligence at the business school and advises EMBA students, and is a frequent speaker at other Columbia University colleges and graduate programs. He was an instructor at New York University's Center for Career, Education, and Life Planning for almost 20 years and was an original Five O'Clock Club counselor, consulting in this national job search advising organization for 21 years.

In addition to his private practice, Ellis has worked in some of the nation's largest human resources and outplacement consulting firms; he also worked in manpower planning and staffing at one of the nation's largest financial services institutions. He is a founding member of the New York Chapter of the Association for Career Management Professionals and holds a BA and MA from New York University.

His articles have appeared in the *National Business Employment Weekly/Wall Street Journal*, *The Five O'Clock Club News*, Columbia Business School Alumni e-newsletter, Vault.com, MBAFreeAgents.com, and he has been interviewed extensively on CNBC and CNN, as well as major newspapers and radio stations.

You can learn more from and about Ellis on his website, www.ellischase.com.